WORLD SHAKERS

INSPIRING WOMEN ACTIVISTS

HELEN WOLFE

World Shakers

Inspiring Women Activists

DO YOU KNOW MY NAME?

Second Story Press

Library and Archives Canada Cataloguing in Publication

Title: World shakers : inspiring women activists / Helen Wolfe.
Names: Wolfe, Helen, 1953-2022, author.
Description: Series statement: Do you know my name?; 2
Identifiers: Canadiana (print) 20220474575 | Canadiana (ebook) 20220474591 |
    ISBN 9781772603224 (softcover) | ISBN 9781772603231 (EPUB)
Subjects: LCSH: Women political activists—Biography—Juvenile literature. | LCSH:
    Women social reformers—Biography—Juvenile literature. | LCSH: Women—
    Political activity—Juvenile literature. | LCSH: Women—Biography—Juvenile
    literature. | LCGFT: Biographies.
Classification: LCC HQ1236 .W65 2023 | DDC j920.72—dc23

Second Story Press gratefully acknowledges the support of the Ontario Arts Council and the Canada Council for the Arts for our publishing program. We acknowledge the financial support of the Government of Canada through the Canada Book Fund.

Conseil des Arts du Canada / Canada Council for the Arts

ONTARIO ARTS COUNCIL
CONSEIL DES ARTS DE L'ONTARIO
an Ontario government agency
un organisme du gouvernement de l'Ontario

Funded by the Government of Canada
Financé par le gouvernement du Canada

Canadä

Published by
Second Story Press
20 Maud Street, Suite 401
Toronto, ON
M5V 2M5
www.secondstorypress.ca

MIX
Paper from
responsible sources
FSC® C103567

For my parents, Toby and Joseph Wolfe, who helped me to be brave at a time when it was not easy for them.

CONTENTS

PAGE 1   INTRODUCTION

PAGE 7   JUDITH HEUMANN: STRONGER TOGETHER

PAGE 18   WOMEN OF AFGHANISTAN: FIGHTING FOR JUSTICE

(ZAHRA MIRZAEI, FAWZIA KOOFI, THE AFGHAN DREAMERS)

PAGE 32   THREE WOMEN BREAKING BARRIERS IN SPORT

(IBTIHAJ MUHAMMAD, FAIROUZ GABALLA, FITRIYA MOHAMED)

PAGE 41   PREGALUXMI ("PREGS") GOVENDER: WOMEN'S AND HUMAN RIGHTS

PAGE 50   LILY EBERT: USING SOCIAL MEDIA TO FIGHT ANTISEMITISM

PAGE 59   MARY TWO-AXE EARLEY: SET MY SISTERS FREE

PAGE 67   CHANGING OUR CONCEPTS OF BEAUTY

(FATIMA LODHI, OLAKEMI OBI, OGO MADUEWESI)

PAGE 78   CLARA HUGHES: RACING THROUGH LIFE'S CHALLENGES

PAGE 90   ALICIA GARZA: USING POWER TO CREATE POSITIVE CHANGE

PAGE 101   ANNIE JIAGGE: CRUSADER FOR WOMEN'S RIGHTS

PAGE 111   ACKNOWLEDGMENTS

PAGE 112   ABOUT THE AUTHOR

INTRODUCTION

Why should you know the names of the women in this book? Most people can easily recite the names of musicians and sports stars, and there are TV shows and YouTube channels dedicated to reporting on the lives of celebrities, sometimes down to the smallest details. So, what is it about the women here that make them worth your time to discover more about them?

The answer is simple. These girls and women are working to make the world better for you—for all of us. Each is fighting for something different, but all have made the leap from quietly accepting existing laws and beliefs, whether they agree with them or not, to being changemakers when they recognize change is needed to improve people's lives. Some of them have even risked their lives to improve those of others. We call these brave individuals *activists*.

Think about this: When someone you know wants to enter a building that has only stairs, and she is in a wheelchair, how do you feel? How do you think she feels? Millions of people around the world confront this same problem every day. Fortunately, in some countries, efforts are made to make all buildings accessible to all people. But those changes have not come by themselves. It took individuals who were willing to fight for their right to enter any building, use a public bathroom, travel on a plane, train, and bus—to live like their friends and neighbors do. Judith Heumann is one of those activists, a change-maker, whose efforts led to the Americans with Disabilities Act, a law that dramatically impacted the lives of all U.S. citizens with physical disabilities. After reading her story, you will remember her name.

Mary Two-Axe Earley, who was born and lived on a reserve in Canada, was also an activist. While all Indigenous people continue to fight for their rights in North America, Indigenous women, because of their gender, have had to battle additional forms of discrimination and injustice. Can you believe that until women like Mary Two-Axe Earley battled for their rights, the law took away their cultural and legal status if they married non-Indigenous men? First Nations men could marry whom they wanted without legal penalty. Sound fair? The women activists didn't think so either, and their daughters and granddaughters have been grateful ever since.

The Holocaust—the organized murder of many millions of people by Hitler and his supporters in Nazi Germany and other parts of Europe during World War II—seems a long time ago. Most of those who survived or were witnesses of that time have died or are in their eighties and nineties. One of those still living is Lily Ebert, who is ninety-five years of age but is determined to stop such atrocities from happening again. She needs to tell her own story to young people so that you will better understand the consequences of hate, which we still see today. And that she does, with the help of her great-grandson, using social media like TikTok and Twitter. Her efforts to fight racism, antisemitism—all forms of prejudice—make this extraordinary, determined woman an activist to remember.

I doubt there is any country in the world where women don't experience inequalities and injustices. A country's history, culture, tradition, and dominant religion still play a large part. In a place like Afghanistan, where the government in power is opposed to women making their own choices, almost all aspects of a woman's daily life like health, education, and civil rights are not controlled by women themselves. But women in Afghanistan want change. This includes groups like the Afghan Dreamers, the extraordinary young women who are advocating that girls in their country be encouraged to study science, technology, engineering, and math. There are also women like Zahra Mirzaei, who is challenging longtime traditions and practices by championing the needs of mothers and newborn babies. She and her colleagues are working to create better health care in a country that is poor and where illiteracy, particularly for women, is high. And Fawzia Koofi, a human rights activist and politician who has survived several assassination attempts, wrote a draft that might have been Afghanistan's first law on the Elimination of Violence Against Women. Their work and their names inspire the millions of women who are fighting for some control in their own lives.

In Canada and the United States, we should not be patting ourselves on the back. Racism, gender inequalities, and harassment in sport are ongoing problems. For instance, it is only in recent years that men of color have been drafted to play in the National Hockey League. Women in sport have consistently been paid less than their male peers, even when they are more successful. Many don't realize that Muslim women who wear hijabs—coverings for their heads—continue to face challenges in their sports. But these women persist in breaking new ground for themselves and for young girls and serious athletes now and in the future. Ibtihaj Muhammad, for instance, became the first American wearing a hijab to win an Olympic medal, and soon after became the inspiration for a new Barbie doll—truly a "world changer" for all little girls wearing hijabs. Being called a "towel head" and other names by her competitors didn't stop Canadian Fairouz Gaballa from becoming an elite long-distance runner at her university. Years after Ethiopian-born Fitriya Mohamed moved to Toronto, she noticed that she was the only Black, Muslim, and hijab-wearing girl playing the sports she loved at her school. As soon as she could, she established a nonprofit women's basketball league for Muslim women, charging no fees so that anyone could join. Not satisfied yet, Fitriya created the Hijabi Ballers, teams of women who play all kinds of ball sports. Aiming to fight discrimination and harassment, these extraordinary change-makers believe that the more often hijab-wearing athletes are seen, the more they will become an accepted part of the sports landscape.

If you have heard of Black Lives Matter, then you should know about Alicia Garza, one of the three women founders of the organization, which has had a tremendous impact on anti-racist activism in many parts of the world. As the child of a mixed-race couple, Alicia was conscious of prejudices from a young age and became active around issues of diversity as she moved into adulthood. But it was the senseless killing of a Black teenager, Trayvon Martin, that galvanized her into reaching "world changer" status. Today, the movement she co-founded is one of the most powerful influences affecting change.

Much of the world has never heard of Annie Jiagge. Born in 1918 to a Black family in Ghana who supported their daughter's desire for an education, Annie used what she learned to help make change for others with less privilege than she had. She started her career as a teacher and later became a lawyer, a judge, and a United Nations representative for her country. Along the way, she also took on roles in numerous other organizations so she could advocate on behalf of the women in her country and the problems they were confronting. As Ghana's leading women's right's activist, Annie helped draft the country's revised constitution in 1991, aiming to ensure that the law applied equally to all citizens. Even before the rise of second-wave feminism in North America, this extraordinary changemaker was fighting for and inspiring women in Africa.

If you follow elite speed skating and cycling, you may know the name Clara Hughes, winner of six Olympic medals for Canada. What you may not know is that her youth was troubled. Alcohol, cigarettes, and marijuana were a regular part of her life as she coped with serious mental health problems, including eating disorders, which followed her into adulthood. With support, Clara not only was able to turn her own life around but also bravely told her story, becoming an advocate for good mental health. While working to change her own behaviors, she argued that mental health problems require support services and networks so that individuals are not expected to deal with them on their own.

If you ask most girls and young women what they worry about, a large percentage of them will say it is how they look. Social ideals around beauty and body image continue to be the cause of self-doubt, depression, insecurity, and even the harassment of women and girls today. Three young activists are working to change attitudes and perceptions so that we can all celebrate ourselves. Starting from a young age, Fatima Lodhi noticed that lighter-skinned women in her home of Pakistan, as well as in Sri Lanka and India, were valued more highly than those with darker skin. Seeing the damage caused by this form of prejudice called *colorism*, Fatima started the Dark is Divine campaign to help South Asian communities re-examine their standards of beauty. Two Nigerian-born women are also challenging traditional standards of beauty. Olakemi Obi, who is a plus-size model, has created a website called Plus is Diverse that features larger women of color from all over the world. Its mission is to increase diverse representation in the fashion industry. When Ogo Maduewesi developed vitiligo, she decided she needed to change attitudes surrounding the disease. Vitiligo is a skin condition that causes loss of skin color in patches. The loss of color is lifelong, and people with this condition regularly face acts of cruelty and harassment from their larger societies. Because of this, Ogo has established support groups, helped enact new government policies surrounding the condition, and even holds a fashion show where all the models have vitiligo. Reading about these women may change your mind about what is beautiful.

Pregs Govender was born in Durban, South Africa, home to one of the largest Indian populations outside of India. For more than thirty years, she lived under apartheid, a racist system of laws and attitudes that was abhorred by most of the world. Growing up under apartheid gave Pregs a strong understanding of the difference between what is just and unjust. After her grandmother told her about Mahatma Gandhi, the Hindu activist who led a nonviolent revolution against the British government that had colonized India, Pregs began to think of herself as an activist against apartheid. From that time, Pregs focused her energies toward making change and fighting injustices of all kinds.

There is one more person you should hear about. Helen Wolfe, who wrote this book and was supposed to write this introduction, was a bit of a world shaker herself. Like Judith in this book, Helen had a lifelong disability. When she was your age, people didn't expect her to accomplish much. People felt sorry for her because she could only walk with crutches, she couldn't go to a "regular" school, she of course couldn't play sports—people believed she couldn't do any of the things they thought were worth doing. But Helen proved everyone wrong. She became an honor student, went to university where, when she graduated, she was the only person with a visible disability out of the five hundred people graduating. Despite many prejudices about her ability to be a classroom teacher, she inspired English Second Language (ESL) students for many years and helped other educators by writing guides about how to use storybooks and novels to help their students. She completed wheelchair marathons, traveled the world, did weight-training, and learned to box. This is the third book Helen has written focusing on women whose names you probably didn't know. You should know her name too.

Hopefully, when you finish reading about these extraordinary women, you will make your own lists of people who deserve to be remembered.

—Margie Wolfe

JUDITH HEUMANN

STRONGER TOGETHER

"I know that having my disability has given me opportunities I wouldn't have had if I hadn't had it…. I know it pushed me to study harder, work harder, and achieve harder…to fight, to change how others saw us." These are the words of American activist Judith "Judy" Heumann, and the "us" are people with disabilities. From the time she was a child and through her adult years, Judy has faced discrimination. She was born to European immigrant parents in Brooklyn, New York, and while she wasn't born with a disability, as a toddler in 1949, she became sick with polio, an epidemic virus that affected children and adults all over the world. Polio can affect the spinal cord, causing weakness or paralysis. Judy was one of forty-three thousand American children who survived the virus but had to learn how to live with a disability. Judy remains a quadriplegic, meaning she has paralysis in her arms and legs and uses a wheelchair to get around.

When Judy was five years old, her mother tried to register her for kindergarten. But at that time, schools would not allow children using wheelchairs to attend school with able-bodied students. Many kids with disabilities needed wheelchairs, walkers, and crutches, of course, but the school boards claimed that these mobility devices were "fire hazards" because they would make the classrooms too crowded and were therefore "unsafe." People with disabilities also need special bathrooms, elevators, ramps, and other devices which are common in public buildings today. But when Judy was growing up, most public buildings like schools didn't have them because the people in charge of those buildings said that it was a waste of money to build them. So, it was difficult—if not impossible—for people who used wheelchairs and other mobility devices to do even day-to-day activities, like go to school, work, or buy groceries. As a result, adults and children with disabilities couldn't leave their homes very much. Students with disabilities either stayed at home, where teachers came to work with them, or they were placed in separate or segregated schools.

Most people at the time thought that these kids didn't need an education like everyone else. Many hold the same attitudes today because despite much talk about the need for diversity and inclusion, issues of disability—like other issues of diversity, even today—remain of secondary importance to lawmakers, businesses, and people without disabilities. Remember, despite the huge number of Americans who are Black and Brown, it wasn't until the giant swell of protest in recent years that the impetus for inclusion and social justice became a priority outside the communities of people of color.

Judy's mother disagreed with this misconception, so she organized with other parents to fight for children with disabilities to be educated in a mainstream public school. Finally, the New York Board of Education told Mrs.

Heumann that her daughter could go to a special education program through the Health Conservation 21 policy. Almost immediately Judy and her mom were confused by what they saw: Judy was supposed to be in Grade 4, yet the other students in her small class were all different ages and grades. Her teacher handed out worksheets that Judy thought were easy, so she would do them quickly and read books while she waited for other students to finish. Judy also worried because one of her classmates was a teenager who had attended the school for a few years but still couldn't read.

Because her school was in the basement of P.S. 219, Judy always heard the footsteps of the non-disabled students as they went about their days in their own school upstairs. Soon, Judy found out that the expectations for them were very different from those for her. While Judy and the other students with disabilities had to be in class for only two or three hours a day, the students upstairs were expected to attend a regular school day from 8:30 a.m. to 3 p.m. These students had to pass all of their school subjects, and if they couldn't, they weren't promoted to the next grade. But the students with disabilities might stay in the same classroom for years. Even though she was just nine years old, Judy knew that her school was very different from the one that kids without disabilities attended. She made friends and enjoyed studying there rather than at home, but she was also bored and believed that she could do well in a mainstream school.

Judy's parents felt the same way. Again, her mother fought the school board, and she became the first student from the Health Conservation 21 program to be transferred to a high school with able-bodied kids. Adjusting to her new environment was difficult. Her daily routine, tests, and exams were harder. The new school building was much bigger and had many more students. Every time the bell rang, and she needed to change classes or use a washroom, Judy had to ask someone she didn't know to push her where she needed to go. She had to get up early and travel an hour and a half on a special bus and then faced the same long ride after school. These long bus rides meant that she never had the chance to join any clubs or participate in after-school activities where she could have made friends. The kids in her high school only saw her wheelchair and not Judy herself, so she felt invisible. But with her parents' encouragement, she worked hard and graduated from high school, even earning an award.

By now, Judy knew she wanted to be a teacher. But like most people with disabilities, Judy faced many roadblocks in the form of discrimination. For example, she was entitled to receive financial help for her education from a government department called Rehab. But that department said she wouldn't get money to study to become a teacher because there had never been a teacher in New York who was a wheelchair user. Judy needed the money, so she lied and told them that she wanted to be a speech therapist instead.

After studying speech therapy and education at Long Island University, in 1970, Judy was ready to apply for her teacher's license. She had passed her school exams but needed to see a doctor and pass a medical exam too. During the medical exam, the doctor asked her embarrassing questions about how she used a bathroom and got dressed, which, of course, had nothing to do with being a teacher. When the doctor asked Judy if she could walk, she was honest and answered that she couldn't. At the end of the interview, the doctor told her to come back for another interview with her crutches to show how she walked. In her second medical exam, Judy refused to bring her crutches to "show" the doctor that she could walk. The doctor wrote the word *insubordinate*, which means "disobedient," on a piece of paper and put it in Judy's file. Three months later, she received a letter from the board of education that said that she wasn't allowed to teach because being unable to walk meant that her classroom would be unsafe.

But nothing was going to stop Judy now. She was determined to fight the board of education's decision. She hired lawyers to help her to prove in court that a person with a disability was qualified, able, and safe to be a teacher. Newspapers wrote articles to encourage and support her. Judy was also interviewed on television about her case and met with people who didn't support her. The issues receiving all of that attention meant that people without disabilities needed to confront the challenges faced by those with disabilities.

In the end, Judy had a court hearing in which the judge ordered the board of education to give her another medical exam. This time, a new doctor gave her a quick exam and apologized for how badly she had been treated. The board of education gave up its case and Judy won, becoming the first person with a physical disability in New York state to become a licensed teacher.

Judy wasn't able to get a teaching job right away, however. Most schools at that time weren't accessible for wheelchair users, and principals frequently used the excuse that they had already hired all the teachers they needed and didn't have a job for her. Eventually, the principal of P.S. 219, the first school that Judy had attended, hired her to teach classes to both students with disabilities and those without. For both groups of students, it was the first time they'd had a teacher with a disability. Judy taught there for three years.

The successful law case created other big changes in her life. Because of the media attention, other disabled people shared with her their stories of being denied accessible transportation, housing, education, and jobs. Judy was deeply affected by this and, working with some of the people she met, she helped to create a group called Disabled in Action and was elected its first president. Becoming a disability rights advocate meant that Judy's mission had grown from improving her own life to improving the lives of others with disabilities. She realized that the best way to do that was to challenge the government to create new laws to protect everyone from discrimination. Judy, together with other disability advocates in the United States, argued that it was vital to add a special section to the Civil Rights Act that would stop discrimination against people with disabilities. Despite the existence of Section 504 of the Rehabilitation Act, which made it illegal for federally funded organizations to discriminate against people with disabilities, physical and social barriers made it hard for people with disabilities to participate fully in American life.

At the same time, Judy began an exciting new life as she moved from her hometown of New York City to attend the University of California in the city of Berkeley. Moving from one side of the country to the other was a huge task for someone with a disability, but for Judy it was well worth it. In Berkeley, she had a better, more active life. With a new motorized wheelchair, she was able to travel easily from one place to another. At school, she studied hard and earned her master's degree in social work, which qualified her to get jobs connected to her activism. At the time Judy attended the university, Berkeley was a center of student unrest, where young people questioned many traditional attitudes, laws, and practices. She made many friends, both with and without disabilities, and she joined other disability advocacy groups. As she became involved with a bigger group of people with various kinds of disabilities, and with other young people fighting for different issues of social justice, Judy learned about the similarities and differences between her and them and realized that it was necessary to improve everyone's life.

Less than a year later, Judy started working as an assistant to a senator in Washington, DC. In American government, each state has two senators who are elected to work in Washington to create and pass laws that protect and help their citizens and all Americans. Judy's new boss, Senator Harrison Williams from New Jersey, was especially concerned with improving education and jobs for people with disabilities. He wanted to pass laws that guaranteed students with disabilities a better education. Of course, this issue was close to Judy's heart. She believed that the "special education" classrooms in elementary school, like the one she had attended, should be closed and that students with disabilities should share the same classrooms with kids without disabilities. This idea of teaching everyone equally in the same classroom is called *integration* or *inclusion*. Using her knowledge and experience, Judy helped to write the Individuals with Disabilities Education Act, which would integrate students with disabilities into schools with their classmates without disabilities.

Becoming an important changemaker didn't prevent Judy from experiencing discrimination. Although she worked in Washington, she sometimes flew back home to New York to visit her parents and family. On one of her flights back to Washington, Judy was about to board the airplane when the airline agent at the counter told her a wheelchair user was not allowed to travel by herself. Judy knew the law and that the agent was wrong. After speaking to two supervisors, she was allowed to board the plane. But just as it was about to take off, several flight attendants said that she needed to get off. She refused to back down and leave the plane. Then, two airport policemen forcibly took her off the plane and into the terminal. When they asked her for identification, Judy showed them a card that proved that she worked for the United States senator from New Jersey, the state where the airport was located. They were embarrassed and let her go. But she had already missed her flight to Washington—and more important, she was upset and angry at how badly she had been treated.

Judy decided that she could not let this horrible treatment go without a fight, so she took the case to court. The judge claimed that this was not discrimination, but Judy continued to fight. Ultimately, the airline settled and paid her money for the embarrassment they had caused her. Judy's confidence and determination were growing—she was only beginning to fight back.

A few months later, the governor of California offered Judy a job in Berkeley, California, which she accepted. She loved being back in the small, accessible city where many groups of people with disabilities were working to help one another. The Rehabilitation Act, which would prohibit employment discrimination against qualified individuals with disabilities for federal government jobs, was about to be passed, but many government departments didn't want that to happen. They thought that spending money to make their buildings accessible and creating new programs and services for disabled people was pointless because they didn't go out in public very much.

These departments didn't understand that people with physical disabilities couldn't use these services because the buildings and services themselves weren't accessible. Even in 1976, many disabled people still couldn't get good education, housing, transportation, or other services. Judy knew all too well that for their lives to change, the American government needed to pass laws that guaranteed them accessibility.

Judy worked with groups that were putting pressure on the government to make these important changes. These groups decided that it was time to organize protests in many cities to force the government to listen to them, and Judy became a leader of the protest in San Francisco, California. She worked hard to bring together groups of people with disabilities and others who experienced discrimination: Black Americans, women, and people with low incomes. Judy realized that when it came to fighting discrimination, the more people who could join the battle, the better.

The protest at a government building in San Francisco was the first time that Judy had organized a big disability rights demonstration. It was also the first time that she had spoken in public about her childhood experiences with discrimination and her strong feelings about changing laws to help people with disabilities. At the end of her speech, Judy said in a clear, strong voice, "We will accept no more discrimination!" This protest was a major turning point in her life and career. She had truly become a disability rights activist. She also asked the protesters to occupy that building, day and night, to show the people in government how serious they were about changing the laws. She was asking them to participate in a "sit-in."

A sit-in is a form of protest used by many groups to get the government and the media to listen to them. For people without disabilities, being in a sit-in isn't complicated. You simply sit down in the area where you are protesting and refuse to leave or move on your own. Many sit-ins last for days and sometimes even weeks. In fact, they often end with the police physically removing protesters from the area. But for people with disabilities to exercise their right to protest, the right to freedom of speech, and the right to assemble enjoyed by other Americans, organizing a sit-in is more challenging. They may need to take medication and require help with their personal care, sleeping arrangements, and special diets.

Judy and other organizers spoke to newspapers, television, and other media about the reasons for the sit-in and to explain to the general public the realities of life for Americans with disabilities. In fact, some newspaper reporters lived with the protesters and wrote about their experiences. There were protests in other American cities, but the one organized by Judy received the most attention because of how well it was organized and the number of participants. More than a hundred people with various disabilities occupied the San Francisco Health Education and Welfare (HEW) office for twenty-six days, until HEW Secretary Joseph Califano signed the legislation.

This new law was only the beginning, The next step was to improve the programs and organizations that were supposed to help people with disabilities. Organizers of these programs were fighting the changes. For example, transit companies said that it would cost too much money to install wheelchair lifts, ramps, and other equipment to make their buses accessible. But Judy and the other activists eventually persuaded them to make these improvements.

Judy also argued that people with disabilities must feel that they have the right to demand what they need. Often, when a student with disabilities spoke to their principal about being unable to attend school because there were no ramps or accessible bathrooms, the principal made that person feel as though they were a complainer or being disruptive. But Judy created programs to encourage people with disabilities to speak up to organizations and people in positions of power who didn't want to listen to them. She also directed the Washington, DC, Department on Disability Services where people could ask for advice about problems that could be settled in court, as Judy had done. This was the first time that people with disabilities were in charge of programs and services to help other people with disabilities.

The United Nations declared 1981 the International Year of the Disabled Person. Judy was already well known to people with disabilities in other countries and was invited to travel around the world to meet them. In Germany, she attended the Paralympics, an international sports event held every four years for people with disabilities. There, she connected with people from every corner of the globe. Through speaking with so many different people, Judy learned that the quality of life for a person with a disability depended greatly on where they lived. For example, Sweden had many programs and services that provided people with disabilities with a good education and job possibilities, accessible transportation and housing, and easy access to public buildings. But in most parts of Africa, South America, and Asia, people with disabilities often had to stay home, just like Judy had done as a child. Inaccessible buildings and discriminatory social beliefs meant that they didn't have any chance to enjoy or improve their lives. Judy realized that there was much work that needed to be done all over the world.

During the 1980s, Judy and other disability rights activists began to understand that it was necessary to have better laws to stop diverse forms of discrimination. For example, they needed to create a law so that a person with a disability couldn't be asked inappropriate or embarrassing questions during an interview, as Judy had experienced during her pre-employment medical exam. This overarching law, which would cover discrimination in many of its different forms, was to be called the Americans with Disabilities Act, or the ADA for short. The important idea behind this law was that citizens with and without disabilities would share the same rights, called *civil rights*. For six years, Judy and the other advocates worked hard fighting the opposition of many private companies and government departments that didn't want to make the effort to change. In 1988, Judy spoke passionately in front of the United States Senate on behalf of the ADA, supported there by seven hundred people with many different disabilities. After many delays in different parts of the government, the Americans with Disabilities Act officially became a law on July 26, 1990. Many would say that for Americans with disabilities, this was world-changing.

After the passing of the ADA, Judy traveled the world, meeting with disabled people and disability advocacy groups to learn about their problems, advise them, and help them. It became clear to her that the issues that Americans with disabilities faced were even more difficult to solve in many developing countries that didn't have the same laws and programs as the United States. For example, because of the ADA, many buildings and facilities in the United States are now accessible, but many developing countries don't have the funds to make these improvements.

Judy spent the last fifty years of her life as a crusader for people with disabilities, yet she also found the time for a wonderful personal life. In 1991, she met Jorge Pineda, a Mexican disability rights advocate, and they married shortly afterward. Judy passed away in 2023 while in her seventies, and was still involved in advising American and international organizations on how to better create an inclusive society up until her death. She had been interviewed many times, including in a TED Talk called "Our Fight for Disability Rights— And Why We're Not Done Yet," which is available online. In 2020, she wrote and published her memoir, *Being Heumann*, in which she told her story and described her lifelong mission to create a fairer world where everyone has the opportunity to succeed. In her book, Judy wrote, "I know that having my disability has given me opportunities I wouldn't have had if I hadn't had it…. I know it pushed me to study harder, work harder, and achieve harder. To travel. I can only know that it was meant to be what it is. I am who I was meant to be…. If you were to acquire a disability tomorrow it would be a change. But I can tell you this: it wouldn't have to be a tragedy," (*Being Heumann*, p. 202). Judy was never someone who felt sorry for herself because she was a wheelchair user. Instead, Judy believed that having a disability gave her many gifts and that we all need to make the most of whatever life has given us.

WOMEN OF AFGHANISTAN

FIGHTING FOR JUSTICE

Like most parts of the world throughout history, Afghanistan has gone through many changes—from times of flourishing arts and culture to times of political upheaval—that greatly affect the lives of all its citizens. But these changes in culture and politics almost always have the greatest impact on women and girls. In the mid-1990s, a group called the Taliban emerged following a breakdown of the government. They began as a small force of Afghan students who wanted to rid the country of the crime and corruption from local armies and the powerful warlords who ruled over them.

As with all Islamist fundamentalist groups, the members of the Taliban believe that every Muslim must follow Islamic principles very strictly according to their beliefs and standards. The majority of Afghans are Muslim—followers of Islam, one of the oldest religions in civilization. As in all religions, followers of Islam have differences in the way they practice their religion. For example, some Muslims wear modest modern clothes that cover their bodies. Many observant Muslim women cover their hair with scarves called hijabs, others cover much of their faces with a cloth called a niqab. Some people pray five times a day, while others do not. Many Muslims observe special dietary laws requiring them to abstain from shellfish, pork, and alcohol. Another important principle of the religion is that men and women who aren't relatives don't have physical contact. Even husbands and wives don't usually hold hands or show affection in public.

Many Afghans approved of the strict Taliban rules and policies, which they thought would bring order and peace to their country. But, once in power, the Taliban passed laws prohibiting women from leaving their homes unless accompanied by male relatives. This prevented girls and women from receiving education and establishing careers. Another restriction was that women had to wear burkas, garments covering their whole body, including their face. If women broke these laws, they faced police violence and arrest.

By 1996, the Taliban had gained control of two-thirds of the country and ruled it from 1997 to 2001. Eventually, they were defeated by a coalition of armed forces from the United States and its allies. Between 2001 and 2021, Afghanistan re-established a democratic government, democratic elections were held, and women re-emerged into public life. But the government remained unstable and collapsed again in September 2021. The U.S. soldiers who had been supporting the regime for twenty years left the country for good. The Taliban quickly regained control of the government and re-imposed its rigid standards.

Although Afghanistan is a challenging country to live in, many girls and women continue to strive to achieve their goals and help their sisters improve their lives. In their own ways, Zahra Mirzaei, Fawzia Koofi, and the Afghan Dreamers Robotics Team have made extraordinary contributions and given hope to Afghan girls and women.

ZAHRA MIRZAEI

CHAMPION OF MOTHERS AND NEWBORN BABIES

Midwifery, the practice where an experienced woman helps an expectant mother to deliver her baby, has a long history all over the world. Sometimes, there is no hospital close by where a doctor can assist at the birth, and sometimes women prefer to give birth at home, in familiar surroundings. In Afghanistan, many women still live in remote and mountainous areas where there are few doctors, and for millennia, midwives have assisted their sisters, friends, and neighbors in childbirth. There, and in other countries, these women did their best to deliver babies safely but sometimes weren't prepared to deal with unexpected problems that could tragically end in mother and baby deaths.

Realizing the need for formal education, many countries now have schools where students receive training to become midwives. Zahra Mirzaei is a young woman who is passionate about midwifery. She was born in 1988 into a traditional large family of ten children, which included eight girls and two boys. When she was a child, her family moved to Iran because of the war in Afghanistan. Even at a young age, Zahra began to understand that her culture treated boys and girls unequally. For example, while boys were expected to study for careers in the trades or other professions, girls usually stayed at home or attended school for just a few years. At the age of eleven, Zahra started to ask serious questions about why the girls in her family weren't able to get an education and achieve the same goals as the boys.

When she was sixteen years old, Zahra and her family returned to Afghanistan and settled in an area where many people were poor and illiterate. There weren't many schools, and she couldn't continue her education. One day, when she was feeling sick, Zahra and her mother went to a neighborhood hospital. While they were waiting for a doctor, she saw a woman dressed in ragged clothes begging a health care worker to help her find a midwife. The health care worker said that it wasn't her job and didn't help the woman. Zahra couldn't believe how unsympathetic one woman could be to another. So, she found the midwives' office in the hospital herself and took the woman there. Although she was young, Zahra's simple act of kindness demonstrated her initiative, compassion, and desire to serve others.

A woman doctor who treated Zahra motivated her to pursue midwifery by answering her questions and encouraging her to continue her education. However, there was no college or university in her area, and her parents thought that it was too dangerous for her to travel far away. As a first step, Zahra enrolled in a midwifery education program in her community. Passionate to learn more about delivering babies, she then earned a college diploma in 2006 and worked as a midwife in hospital births and a trainer of other midwives.

Working daily in a hospital, Zahra was alarmed by what she saw. It seemed more like a factory. In her first year in practice, one hundred fifty babies were delivered by only five midwives. Sometimes, women would be left alone to give birth in hallways or washrooms because there weren't enough hands to help them. Midwives didn't have the time and energy to offer emotional support to the mothers.

Most Afghan people don't have access to the same kind of medical care that people living in the Global North often have. As a midwife, Zahra has felt both the joy and the sadness of working in a country with very limited resources. For example, Zahra can't forget the first time she helped a woman give birth when Zahra was still a student. The woman had already had five pregnancies but none of her babies had survived. Zahra helped to safely deliver a healthy baby and, of course, the mother was extremely grateful. However, Zahra can also tell tragic stories. Once, a mother of four who had already given birth to her fifth child by herself came to her bleeding and in shock. Zahra called for help, but it was too late, and tragically, the woman died.

In 2014, Zahra joined and helped to coordinate the Afghan Midwives Association, which gave her the opportunity to talk with other women about the challenges of doing lifesaving work. In 2016, this ambitious, caring woman earned a bachelor of science university degree in midwifery. Eventually, through her hard work, she became president of the Afghan Midwives Association and established birthing centers throughout the country, which provide respectful, compassionate care. Each center employs about seventy-five midwives and safely delivers twenty-five to thirty new babies every day.

Zahra also learned more about the many problems faced by midwives throughout the country, such as long, exhausting work hours, low salaries, and little opportunity to improve their medical knowledge. But the most horrible situation was the danger from the Taliban or other armed groups who disrespect and abuse women. Such groups have attacked health care facilities and sexually assaulted female staff.

During 2019 and 2020, the government became even more unstable, launching Afghanistan's health care system into chaos. In 2019, there were 119 attacks by terrorist groups on health care facilities. In May 2020, there was a massacre at a maternity ward that Zahra had helped to establish. Among the dead was a midwife colleague of hers named Maryam Noorzad. She was killed because she refused to leave a woman in labor alone. After the baby was born, the gunman also killed the mother and the baby.

In the summer of 2021, Zahra realized that the Afghan government was going to collapse and that she and her three children were in great danger from the Taliban. In addition to the risk posed by her midwife work, Zahra comes from the Hazara tribe, a predominantly Shiʻa Muslim ethnic group that has experienced many years of discrimination and persecution. Thousands of Hazaras had been killed by the Taliban. She also understood that because of their prejudices toward women, the Taliban would never accept the lifesaving work that she was doing.

On August 23, 2021, Zahra left Afghanistan with her three children. Like tens of thousands of Afghans fleeing the country, they spent hours hiding near the airport before being airlifted to the country of Qatar. From there, the family transferred to a refugee camp in Southern Spain. But Zahra is not content to remain a refugee and is preparing to start a new stage in her life. She has been accepted to study global maternal health at the University of London and is waiting for a special visa to travel and live in England.

Even though she is now far from home, Zahra continues to support the Afghanistan Midwives Association, which she worked so hard to build. When she is asked why she chose to leave her beloved country, Zahra says simply that she needed to give her children a better future.

Zahra Mirzaei is a young, accomplished woman. Clearly, no matter where she lives, she will continue to use her skill and ever-expanding knowledge to assist women to give birth to healthy babies.

FAWZIA KOOFI

RISKING HER LIFE FOR WOMEN'S RIGHTS

In North America and Europe, women have the right to run for political office and speak out about issues, such as poverty, homelessness, education, and employment, that affect their constituents: the people they represent. Although they consistently face sexist harassment on social media, physical attacks are rare. Unfortunately, female politicians in Afghanistan face enormous obstacles when doing the same work.

Fawzia Koofi was born into a polygamous family in Afghanistan. Many such families have one husband and father but several wives and mothers. They usually also have a lot of children. Fawzia's father had seven wives. In

Afghanistan, female children are often not as respected or as valued as boys are. The day that Fawzia was born in 1975, she was rejected by her parents and was left out in the sun to die, although her mother then changed her mind and rescued the baby. Perhaps it was this awful beginning of being unwanted that created in Fawzia sympathy for others in need of help.

Supported by her mother, Fawzia became the only girl in her family to get an education. Originally, she wanted to study to be a doctor but was forced to leave school after the Taliban took control of the government in 1996. In 2001, after the Taliban fell, Fawzia was able to return to school and graduated from Preston University in Pakistan with a master's degree in business management.

Although her education was in business, Fawzia was interested in getting experience working with different groups in society. She helped refugees who fled their homes because of war, women who had no family support, and children. From 2002 to 2004, she worked as a child protection officer with UNICEF, the United Nations International Children's Emergency Fund. UNICEF is a worldwide organization created after World War II to rescue children who had been affected by war, disease, or natural disasters. Today, UNICEF provides children with food and shelter, and helps them to relocate and start new lives.

Eventually, Fawzia entered politics. The newly elected democratic government motivated girls to get an education. Fawzia traveled the country to publicize a successful Back to School campaign. In the parliamentary elections of 2005, she was elected to Afghanistan's National Assembly and then served as the first woman deputy speaker of Parliament in the history of the country. She was reelected as a member of Parliament in the election in 2010, along with sixty-eight other women, another groundbreaking event in a country that had denied girls and women their basic human rights for so long.

As a member of Afghan Parliament, Fawzia focused on three areas: education, health care, and women's rights. She spoke out against the inequalities facing Afghans living in the mountains and other isolated areas, and one of her first actions was to introduce and work to pass laws authorizing the building of roads to connect remote villages to education and health care facilities. She also pushed the government to provide students with access to good schools with qualified teachers, and she worked to provide less formal, but critical basic literacy education for adults and children. Fawzia also took the initiative to raise private money to build girls' schools in remote provinces.

Fawzia has advocated for several issues to benefit girls and women. In 2009, she wrote a draft of a document of her country's first law on Elimination of Violence Against Women. The Afghan Parliament then voted for this important document to become a law and part of the country's constitution, which guarantees the rights of every citizen. With the Taliban return in 2021, the law's implementation was discontinued.

Fawzia's life has been filled with significant challenges and dangers, which have made her contributions even more significant. Like many Muslim women, Fawzia followed the ancient custom and accepted an arranged marriage to a man named Hamid who was an engineer and a chemistry professor. They had two daughters together. Hamid was imprisoned by the Taliban and contracted tuberculosis. In many countries, children get vaccinations for tuberculosis and even if they get sick, those infected can typically access medical care and fully recover. Hamid was released from prison in 2003 but sadly died shortly afterward. So, Fawzia is a single mother who lives with her two daughters, who are now in their early twenties. There have also been many opposed to her work for women's rights who will do anything to stop her. Fawzia has survived several assassination attempts, the first one on March 8, 2010, which happened to be International Women's Day. The last attempt was in August 2020, when she was shot in the arm by a gunman in the capital city of Kabul.

In the 2014 election, Fawzia wanted to run for president of the country. The changes she proposed during her campaign were to improve the rights for women, ensure education for all Afghan children, and fight against political corruption. To stop her from running, the Afghan election commission changed the date to register as a candidate to October 2013. The minimum age to run for president of Afghanistan is forty years old, but Fawzia was too young at the age of thirty-nine. Instead, she ran and was reelected as a Member of Parliament in 2014 but lost her important role as deputy speaker. She served as chairperson of Afghanistan's Women's and Human Rights Commission. In 2021, Fawzia was one of only four women on a twenty-one–member team assigned to represent the Afghan government to negotiate peace talks with the Taliban.

Despite attempts to silence her, Fawzia has achieved many milestones, both for herself and for women in her country. Recently, she was nominated for the Nobel Peace Prize, which acknowledges people who have made life-long contributions to human rights and their societies. She has also written an autobiography called *The Favored Daughter: One Woman's Fight to Lead Afghanistan into the Future*, which tells the story of her life through her child-hood, education, and involvement in politics. The book also includes moving letters that she wrote to her two daughters about her mission to represent and improve the rights of Afghan women.

After the Taliban again seized control of the government in August 2021, Fawzia left the country and visited the United Nations in New York as a woman in exile, making her one of the hundred thousand Afghans who have left the country. In New York, she gave several interviews where she has called for humanitarian aid to assist women and other vulnerable groups to leave Afghanistan. After leaving the country, she lived in hotel rooms in Europe, trying to find a home for herself and her daughters. Each day, Fawzia gets hundreds of text messages from Afghan women hoping she can help them, but she often doesn't have easy answers for them.

Fawzia has made a tremendous contribution to improving the lives of girls and women in her native country. Unfortunately, as for many Afghan people from all walks of life, the Taliban's control has made it impossible for her to continue to live and work there. However, her dedication, gifts, and accomplishments are without question. Only time will tell where she and her family will settle and what additional amazing things she will accomplish.

THE AFGHAN DREAMERS

BEATING THE ODDS TO EXCEL IN SCIENCE

Girls in Afghanistan face an uphill battle in getting a good education to ensure they have a positive future. The country is currently one of the world's most hostile places for girls and women. Most don't have the opportunity to learn to read and write well enough to do daily tasks, which, of course, continues to make them dependent on the men in their families. However, there is a small group of Afghan girls who have succeeded far beyond anyone's expectations.

The acronym STEM stands for science, technology, engineering, and math. Throughout history, around the world, female students have not been encouraged to study these fields. Traditionally, when compared to boys, girls were thought to have more sensitive, intuitive, and compassionate personalities, which were considered more suited to jobs as teachers, social workers, or psychologists. On the other hand, boys have often been encouraged to take math and science courses, which eventually lead them to careers in the STEM disciplines. But recently, these gender-based attitudes are changing. Parents, teachers, and guidance counselors are now encouraging female high school students to tackle courses in all disciplines and that can lead them to a wider range of career options, including those in science, engineering, math, and technology.

Countries like Afghanistan don't always have the money to invest in schools, teachers, and materials offering STEM courses, and the resources they do have are reserved for boys. However, in some countries, private companies and foundations that have recognized talented female students have stepped in to fund educational programs for them. In 2017, Roya Mahboob and an organization called the Digital Citizen Fund created a STEM program for seven girls between the ages of fourteen and seventeen. This imaginative team is dedicated to building innovative robots, which they then enter into competitions all over the world. This all-girl robotics team, now captained by Somaya Faruqi, are clearly the underdogs in comparison to other teams who have much more support, earning them the nickname the "Afghan Dreamers."

Because of the poverty and violence in their country, the Afghan Dreamers faced many challenges in traveling to international robotics competitions. Their first one happened to be in Washington, DC, in the United States. The girls had to travel several hundred kilometers from their home in Hera to get visas from the U.S. embassy in Kabul, the capital city. But the government denied them their visas without giving them any reason. Afghan Americans protested, so then-President Donald Trump intervened, and the American embassy gave them special status to compete. When the Dreamers returned from their first international competition with the silver medal "for courageous achievement," their families and communities offered more support. Their accomplishment became widely known and created hope and pride in Afghanistan, especially among girls and women. The team has gone on to win several international robotics competitions.

Since they began, the girls have competed in many international robotics competitions and won accolades for their wonderfully useful creations. For example, they won an Entrepreneur Challenge at a festival in Estonia for developing a solar-powered robot that could assist farmers in completing their never-ending physical labor. Because the Afghan economy depends heavily on agriculture, this innovation could help farmers work faster and more efficiently. They would earn higher incomes and greatly improve their families' standard of living.

Since 2020, the COVID-19 pandemic has changed the world. Especially before the development of the antiviral medications, vaccines, and boosters to fight the virus, COVID-19 patients had to rely on artificial breathing machines called ventilators to treat and hopefully survive the illness. However, these machines are expensive and often there haven't been enough of them to meet the global demand. Following a call from the government of Herat province, the Afghan Dreamers developed a low-cost robot ventilator out of used car parts. The original machine was reproduced and used to save lives all over the country.

The Afghan Dreamers have won many accolades and awards for their courage and extraordinary skills. For example, they were selected as UNICEF's Hidden Heroes. *Forbes*, a major business magazine, has recognized their achievement as part of its 30 Under 30 in Asia award. *Teen Vogue* magazine has told their story as part of its "21 under 21, in 2021" edition and superior examples of "Young People Shaping Tomorrow." Inspired by the Afghan Dreamers, the University of Kabul is hoping to create a Dream Institute that will provide a world-class STEM education to Afghan students and promote access for women in those fields. It is hoping to start both a STEM high school and a university degree program, providing new opportunities, especially for women. Finally, in 2021, the team won the First Global Competition Judges Award and its team captain accepted the award at the United Nations on March 8, International Women's Day.

In August 2021, the Afghan government collapsed, and the Taliban extremists quickly took control. The Dreamers wanted to stay but understood that they would not be allowed to continue their education or develop more robotics inventions. The Dreamers were more fortunate than most Afghans. Business sponsors applied to the nearby country of Qatar so that they could continue their education at the University of Doha and other world-renowned universities.

Then, Mexico invited them to immigrate there, and five of the girls accepted. After they arrived, the Dreamers felt that they were free to issue this statement: "We are happy that today we are safe, not only because of ourselves, but here we can be the voice of thousands of girls who want to be safe in Afghanistan and who want to continue their education to make their dreams come true.... The rule of the government is a mockery and an insult to Islam."

A few teammates have remained in Afghanistan or gone to the United Arab Emirates and Europe.

The Taliban has ordered high schools and universities to remain open but only to admit male students.

THREE WOMEN BREAKING BARRIERS IN SPORT

We all come from different religious and cultural backgrounds, each with our own unique customs, from the way we season our food to the clothes we choose to wear. Some girls and women who follow the Muslim faith wear a hijab, which is a scarf that covers the hair, neck, and shoulders. To them, it represents modesty, privacy, and moral values. For Muslim girls, wearing a hijab is a sign that they are becoming young women. Another reason is that they want to show their pride in their culture and traditions. Some people misunderstand and think that these women are forced to wear hijabs, but that's not always true. Girls and women choose to wear hijab as part of their religious practice and to maintain modesty in public. In this chapter you will learn about three amazing North American women athletes who proudly wear their hijabs when they are competing despite official resistance.

IBTIHAJ MUHAMMAD

OLYMPIC MEDALIST

When she was a child, Ibtihaj Muhammad noticed that her dolls didn't look like her because they weren't wearing hijabs like she was. So, she decided to cut tiny pieces of cloth to make little hijabs for them. Not surprisingly, this creative, independent girl became the first American Muslim athlete wearing a hijab to win an Olympic medal.

Ibtihaj is a Black woman who was born and grew up in New Jersey. Her parents decided that they wanted their whole family to convert to Islam when she and her four siblings were young. Her father was a police officer and her mother was an elementary special education teacher. Ibtihaj's parents always encouraged her to be physically active, but according to Islamic tradition, wanted her to choose a sport where she could dress modestly and also wear her hijab. She participated in different sports in school, but it was always challenging. For example, her mother, Denise, had to alter all her sports uniforms to add both sleeves and coverings for her legs. When she was thirteen, Ibtihaj and her mother saw a high school fencing team practicing outside. Because fencers wear long sleeves, pants, and a helmet, she saw immediately that she could participate in this sport, while at the same time respecting her religion. So, she decided to join her school fencing team.

Ibtihaj loved the sport, kept improving, and a few years later joined the Westbrook Foundation, a special program that uses fencing to encourage participation in sports and community involvement while creating confidence in students from different cultural backgrounds. After being recognized for her talent, she was invited to train in an elite program for athletes in New York City. From then on, her fencing skills improved rapidly. Ibtihaj was also a bright, hardworking student who won a scholarship to Duke University, where she continued fencing for her college team. In 2005, she became a Junior Olympics champion and took a step closer to fulfilling her Olympic dream.

In 2010, Ibtihaj became a member of the United States National Fencing team and has won five medals in international competitions. When she qualified for the 2016 Olympics, she attracted a lot of attention as the United States' first athlete who chose to wear a hijab in competition. In her television interviews at the Olympics, she made the controversial comment that the United States was a dangerous place for Muslims. She had good reason for her opinion. Just like those from many other communities, Muslim people have been the targets of violence and discrimination ranging from being attacked, robbed, and harassed, to facing prejudice in getting a good education and jobs. Because some individuals don't understand why Muslim women wear hijabs, Ibtihaj herself experienced situations in which she was treated badly or unjustly. Although she is grateful for the support she received, she hasn't backed down in her criticisms of the United States. She went on to win the team saber bronze medal, becoming the first American Muslim woman to win an Olympic medal.

After her success at the Olympics, Ibtihaj became busy with new projects. In 2014, she and her siblings started a clothing company called Louella. The difference between Louella and other fashionable clothes is that they are modest. The clothes are colorful, well-made, and stylish, but cover all parts of the body, which is appropriate for observant Muslim women and any other woman who prefers to dress modestly. Ibtihaj is also a sports ambassador for a program called Empowering Women and Girls Through Sport Initiative and has traveled to different countries to talk about how important it is for girls and women to participate in sports as part of getting a well-rounded education.

Another fun accolade came from Barbie manufacturer Mattel. Barbie dolls have been around for over sixty years, and during that time, young girls have been able to buy and appreciate different kinds of Barbies to reflect changing, more modern ideas about women. For example, girls can buy a Barbie who uses a wheelchair, a Barbie police officer, and a Barbie astronaut. In 2017, the Mattel toy company introduced a series of new dolls that depicts still more women in modern life. Echoing Ibtihaj's childhood experience with dolls, two of the dolls wear a hijab, including Barbie the fencer, who was inspired by Ibtihaj.

Like other successful athletes, Ibtihaj feels grateful for the opportunities that she has had and is now committed to giving back. For example, in 2019, she became a global ambassador for the Special Olympics, a worldwide program that helps kids and adults with developmental disabilities to participate in many sports. Special Olympics athletes partner with coaches who train them to excel in sports. They not only become proficient in the sport but also develop self-confidence and pride in their achievements.

Ibtihaj made the decision not to compete in the 2020 Olympics, choosing to retire from competition and instead focus on sharing her talents in other ways. She explained her decision with these words: "It has always been my intention to transcend sport and to reach people outside of fencing." In 2018, Ibtihaj wrote a book for adults about her journey to an Olympic medal called *PROUD: My Fight for an Unlikely American Dream*, as well as a children's book *The Proudest Blue: A Story of Hijab and Family*, which has become a bestseller. *Time* magazine has also included her on a list of its "100 Most Influential People," recognizing her important contributions and all the great things she will do in the future.

Ibtihaj is still a young woman who has already achieved amazing goals in sports, education, and helping and motivating others. She has proven that athletes are not just people who care about their sports but also thoughtful, caring individuals who use their talents and voices to address concerns impacting the larger world.

FAIROUZ GABALLA

FIGHTING DISCRIMINATION

Muslim athlete Fairouz Gaballa is from Prince Edward Island (PEI), a beautiful province on the East Coast of Canada. While much of Canada has very diverse populations of people from different religions and traditions, tiny PEI is mostly populated by those from Christian European countries. So, what did an Egyptian-born Muslim girl like Fairouz experience there?

Like many observant Muslim girls, Fairouz began wearing a hijab when she was a teenager. Wearing it made her feel more connected to her culture and religion. But when she started wearing her hijab, her life changed a lot. Fairouz went from having lots of friends to no friends at all. People assumed that she was a refugee from a faraway country who didn't speak English. In fact, the opposite was true. As a young child, Fairouz immigrated to Canada from Egypt with her family and speaks English fluently. But after she started wearing her hijab, other kids started to call her "towel head" and a terrorist. She also noticed that her teachers treated her differently and weren't as friendly.

Fairouz and her sister were involved in track and field and martial arts. at high school sports competitions, Fairouz saw other women athletes wearing hijabs, but never anyone from PEI. After only one year as a runner in her high school, she made the women's distance running team at the University of PEI in 2020. But she's still the only athlete wearing a hijab. Sadly, she continues to face discrimination from those who don't understand Islam and its principles. But Fairouz does have an important supporter—her university running coach. He expects all of his athletes to work as a team and be accepting of one another's religious and cultural differences. Gradually, her teammates have begun to treat her as a valued team member.

Fairouz is happy to be a role model for any young girl or woman wearing a hijab who refuses to be stopped by other people's prejudices. In fact, she thinks that those who try to stop her are not very secure about their own culture and traditions. Some people smile at her as a symbol of diversity; others call out insults. But, she told Ici Radio-Canada, "I'm happy to prove bigots wrong and I'm happy to smile at people who call me 'towel head' as I run past them."

Fairouz is now studying for a bachelor's degree in English and psychology, and continues competing in long-distance running, but she also makes time for other interests. For example, she is the managing editor of her university newspaper, *The Cadre*. She also loves art and to create animation, digital illustrations, and paintings. Unlike most runners, Fairouz actually prefers to run in the winter rather than in warm weather. She also loves creative writing and has had a poem called "Lullabies" published. Although she is considered an elite athlete, she's unsure whether it will lead to the Olympics. Long-distance runners don't reach their peak or best performance years until they are at least thirty years old, so she has a few years to perfect her athletic ability and decide if she wants to pursue higher athletic goals. Already, Fairouz has certainly proven to be a wonderful barrier-breaker.

FITRIYA MOHAMED

CHANGING THE LOOK OF THE BASKETBALL COURT

When she was ten years old, Fitriya Mohamed's family immigrated to Canada from Ethiopia. They decided to live in Toronto, the country's largest city, which has residents from all over the world, bringing with them their diverse traditions, experiences, and cultures. But of course, everything still seemed very different and strange for Fitriya's family. Probably one of her biggest challenges was that she had never been to school. When she arrived, Fitriya was placed in Grade 5. Perhaps you can relate to the challenge of attending school for the first time without understanding English. But she worked hard to learn the language and make a space for herself in Canadian culture, and so she participated in as many after-school activities as she could.

While she was in gym class, Fitriya loved to see all the sports—they were like a new world to her. In Ethiopia, she could only watch her boy cousins play soccer from the sidelines as girls were not encouraged to participate in sports or any physical activities. She also appreciated how easily and freely her classmates moved and the friendly competition that existed between them. In elementary school, her physical education teacher didn't like her just sitting watching everyone else, so she encouraged Fitriya to get off the bench and play. As she gradually learned to speak English and could communicate better with her classmates, Fitriya enjoyed playing basketball, soccer, and badminton because she could feel completely comfortable wearing her hijab when she played.

When she got to high school, Fitriya tried out for all three sports, which were coached by the same man, Greg Brohman. In her opinion, working with this special coach changed the way that she saw herself. He never treated her differently because she was Muslim and wore her hijab. By her last year of high school, she played all three sports so skillfully that she was voted her school's Female Athlete of the Year. Unfortunately, Fitriya's mother didn't really understand or approve of her daughter's love of sports. She would ask, "What will basketball practice do for you?" She wanted Fitriya to focus just on her education.

When she finished high school, Fitriya enrolled in a program to study sports management at Brock University. In the beginning, her mother disagreed with her because she wasn't sure that it was a practical choice. She wanted her daughter to study for a more traditional career that she better understood. But she soon accepted Fitriya's decision. As she continued playing sports at university, Fitriya observed that the players didn't represent the cultural diversity of Canada. In fact, she was the only Black woman, the only Muslim, and the only woman wearing a hijab. Obviously, women like herself were not being encouraged to play sports. She decided that her mission was to encourage more of them to participate, both for their physical fitness and to feel more a part of Canadian society. She was also inspired by Muslim women athletes around the world, such as Bilqis Abdul-Qaadir, who for four years fought the International Basketball Federation's rule that banned religious head coverings from the court (the Federation ruled in her favor in 2017).

As part of her new mission, Fitriya started a nonprofit basketball league for Muslim women. An organization or a club is nonprofit when it is not supposed to earn any profit. It usually just covers its costs. If it's a nonprofit sports team, usually the participants play for free or at very low cost. Fitriya thought that it was important for the league to be nonprofit because new immigrants often don't have a lot of money for necessities and can't afford extras such as sports clubs. A neighborhood boys and girls club and community center gave them a place to practice. The Muslim Women's Basketball League was scheduled to start in the summer of 2020, inviting participants from the greater Toronto area. Unfortunately, the COVID-19 virus has made it difficult for the league's teams to play each other regularly. Like many other activities that were postponed or canceled, it will continue once the pandemic has resolved. Fitriya's big dream is to start Muslim women's basketball leagues all over the world to connect women through sports.

Fitriya has also created an organization called the Hijabi Ballers that encourages and celebrates the athletic ability of Muslim girls and women. "Ballers" not only play basketball but any "ball" sport. This Toronto-based group aims also to increase the participation and representation of Muslim women in all sports programs in Toronto. The name Hijabi Ballers represents three ideas: being a Muslim with faith, an athlete, and a boss. Being a "baller" is to be in control of your own future and capable of making key choices and decisions in your life.

The organization is committed to providing opportunities for women to try new sports. Recently, we have seen more hijab-wearing women as newscasters and in other roles on television, and the Ballers are encouraging Muslim women to be in sports media programs. The Ballers are also actively involved in developing partnerships with allies, such as coaches, parents, and community leaders who will help Muslim women to achieve these goals. Building these teams of helpers will mean that Muslim women may not face as much discrimination and will have greater opportunities to succeed. Female Muslim athletes have needs that can differ from those of other women competitors, and the Ballers have created a toolkit with suggestions for the coaches and other helpers who work with them.

Fitriya Mohamed was a young immigrant who faced challenges in adjusting to Canadian life. She has realized that playing sports has been a great outlet for her abilities, as it has allowed her to feel more fully a part of Canadian society. She also feels a great responsibility to help other girls and women like herself to become empowered by sports and to explore what sports can do to help them meet their goals. Perhaps most importantly, she has found a way to achieve these goals while maintaining her religious and cultural beliefs.

PREGALUXMI ("PREGS") GOVENDER

WOMEN'S AND HUMAN RIGHTS

When people are called *insubordinate*, they are seen as individuals who refuse to obey orders from their superiors. Often, insubordinates believe that the order is wrong and that they need to make their own decisions. Throughout history, insubordinates have also often been courageous people who see injustices and do everything they can to fight them.

Pregs Govender calls herself an insubordinate. She was born and raised in South Africa, which is now a very multiracial country. For much of its history, the area was ruled by different African kingdoms whose influence and trade relationships often stretched across the whole continent and into South and East Asia. In the 1600s, Dutch traders established the first permanent European settlement in South Africa, which over time brought more white Europeans to the region. Although Europeans were in the minority, a series of wars saw the British take control of much of the area. Having also colonized India, the British moved many people from India to South Africa, where they were forced to work as indentured servants and laborers following the abolition of the slave trade in British colonies in the early nineteenth century.

Indentured servitude is a form of labor in which a person has to work without pay for a number of years, sometimes as a way to repay a debt or as a form of punishment. In many ways, indentured servitude was basically a new form of slavery, and it was eventually outlawed. South Africa has a complicated history of race relations, and this continued into the twentieth century. From 1948 until 1992, the country was governed by a cruelly racist system called apartheid, where ruling power was in the hands of white people called Afrikaners. Although the white South Africans were only a small percentage of the population, they controlled the majority population with an iron fist, often using violence to maintain power. A rigid system of laws and regulations segregated the Black population and other people of color, with the intention of keeping them poor and without power.

Pregs Govender was born into an Indian family of five in 1960 in Durban, a culturally rich city that has one of the largest populations of Indians outside India. Her older family members originally came from India and followed the Hindu religion. Pregs was lucky because several family members taught her important traditions as she was growing up. Her grandmother, Aya, would tell her stories about their homeland and took her to films where Pregs learned about her Indian history and culture. She heard about Mahatma Gandhi, the spiritual Hindu activist whose nonviolent protests forced the British to leave India so that it could become an independent country. Her grandmother worked quietly with many organizations to improve the lives of Indian South Africans. Pregs's mother, a teacher, had a great love of reading and introduced Pregs to classic books.

But school life was not always easy for Pregs. Her family was Hindu, but schools in South Africa were based on Christianity, the religion of the ruling Afrikaners.

Also, her teachers would pick on her work habits, calling her a "problem child." Because of this terrible treatment she developed a stutter. Pregs would stumble over her words, and it was hard for her to speak in full sentences. Her teacher would just yell at her to speak up.

From a young age, Pregs realized that she and other racialized students were treated unfairly. She wanted to fight back. One day, when she was in Grade 7, her teacher asked her to stand up and sing the apartheid state's national anthem—she refused. Pregs even nudged the student in front of her and said, "Sit down. Pass it on," so that none of the students in the class sang the anthem. In the same year, she also wrote her first political speech, which criticized apartheid, and she read it to the class. Pregs's teacher refused to believe that someone so young would have such strong views to write this kind of speech, so she accused Pregs's father of writing it for her.

Pregs was developing a keen sense of right and wrong and a social conscience. Her father told her about a plan to raise money for political prisoners in South Africa, and she told the students who helped her that the money was for a good cause. One of her teachers tried to stop Pregs by reporting her to the school principal as a troublemaker. When the principal confronted her, Pregs told her that money was being raised and donated to a much less controversial "milk fund," which provided milk at school for children whose families had low incomes. Ultimately, all the money that was collected did end up going to the milk fund and not for political prisoners.

Pregs's older brother, Daya, helped her to become more aware of the problems of Black people in South Africa. When he was studying to be a doctor, the police broke up a demonstration organized by Black students. Daya was upset that Indian students didn't join the protest. Pregs soon realized that anyone who wasn't white or Afrikaner was considered an outsider and faced discrimination. She only needed to go into her neighborhood and see signs restricting access to facilities, such as "Indian," "Colored," "African," and "White" and hear the term "non-whites," which referred to people of color like her. In the news and in public conversation, "non-whites" were always portrayed as troublemakers who were blamed for all the country's problems and who needed to be controlled.

In every place where discrimination and inequality occur, university students often organize and participate in protests against injustices, and South African students during apartheid did as well. They organized protests in part to show just how many people were willing to fight against the racist practices of the ruling powers, because as the saying goes, there is strength in numbers. Another reason was to gain public support. During apartheid, the government controlled the media, which includes radio, television, and newspapers, so it was difficult for any uncensored news to be reported to South African people.

When she was studying at the University of Durban-Westville, Pregs participated in her first big protest rally with other university students. She and the other women protesters attended their rally on buses. While they were boarding those buses, government soldiers sprayed water hoses on them, yelled insults and swear words, and shot and hit them with guns and bayonets. But Pregs and the other protesters courageously continued on to their demonstration.

When she was twenty-one years old, Pregs began her teaching career. From the beginning, her opinions and ideas were different from her colleagues. For example, she was against the old-fashioned method of simply having students memorize information and then repeat it back, called *rote learning*. She understood that rote learning was not helping them to think. Another old-fashioned, cruel practice that teachers used was corporal punishment. If students gave wrong answers or were not well-behaved, teachers were allowed to hit them with straps or sticks. But Pregs refused to use physical punishment and instead was patient with her students. Pregs continued to teach in different schools for several years. She would often be transferred from one school to another, but not because she disliked her class or was a bad teacher. She just refused to discipline by hitting them. She also treated each student fairly and encouraged them to do their best. The last principal that she worked with tried to bully her into using the old-fashioned teaching methods that Pregs hated. So, Pregs decided to quit her final teaching job and resign from the school board in Durban where she had taught for several years. Instead, she began teaching at university and learned more about challenges faced by women and people of color.

Pregs's life changed in other ways. She married and soon had two children. Pregs tried to settle into her new life but found that it was disappointing. It takes a lot of work to keep a home clean and organized, but her husband had the old-fashioned idea that housework was "women's work." So, she had to take care of the children, cook, and clean all by herself. He never helped her, even though she was also teaching full-time.

But she remained interested in the problems faced by women and other oppressed groups. At this time, Pregs began thinking of herself as a feminist who believed that women should have the same human rights as men. For many years, feminists have been working to demand that their governments and other organizations improve the status of women. In 1982, Pregs and a group of feminists began *SPEAK*, the first feminist magazine in South Africa. She also began to attend meetings with women in their own homes where they could take care of their children and discuss issues at the same time. Together, they were able to determine the similarities of the challenges faced by South African women in general and those faced by the racialized groups, such as Black and Indian people. The more she heard and read, the more Pregs realized that the best way to make changes was for many groups to work together.

Since 1977, March 8 has been celebrated as International Women's Day by many countries all over the world. In 1982, Pregs participated in her first International Women's Day march, along with 20,000 Black, Asian, and white South African feminists.

Because of her experience, Pregs had so much understanding of women's challenges that she represented South African feminists in many national and international meetings and conferences, including the 1995 UN conference on women, held in Beijing. She continued to develop ideas for improvements, inspired by what women were achieving in other countries. At this time, her husband also confessed that he had been having relationships with other women. Since Pregs had been unhappily married for a long time, she decided to divorce her husband. Today, many kids have divorced parents, and either take turns living with each parent or live with one single parent. But at that time, single parents were often criticized for not having a stable and happy home. Also, single women tend to earn much less than men, and it would be a struggle for Pregs to make enough money to support herself and her children.

She was involved in another challenge. South Africa has a lot of clothing factories where many Black and Indian women work. Usually, workers are poorly paid and work very long hours. The government treated these workers as though the small wage that they earned did not go to support the family but simply was just spending money. In fact, these women's husbands often didn't have jobs, so the women's wages supported their entire families. Because she wanted to bring justice to these Indian and Black women, Pregs started working with the garment workers' union, which was supposed to protect the worker's rights and prevent them from being hurt by their employers. For instance, it was common for Afrikaner bosses to accuse their female workers of stealing clothing, and they would search them without their permission. If the women refused, they could lose their jobs. Pregs met with factory workers who told humiliating stories of being searched in front of managers who didn't take their complaints seriously. Later in the same week, all of the garment workers walked out in protest. Gradually, the workers thought of different ways to stop the searches, and eventually they and their managers signed an agreement stopping them altogether.

Pregs soon became one of the union leaders, and the only woman in that position. She organized meetings and led discussions between different groups of women workers. But the Indian men in the union didn't like or trust her. In fact, one of them, whom she had known for a long time, attacked her verbally and physically. Pregs decided to formally complain about his treatment and ask that he be disciplined. At the meeting to discuss her complaint, she was told that the attack was her fault because she had made the man angry. To make matters even worse, the male trade unionists stopped talking or meeting with her. Pregs wanted to introduce programs to help the garment workers, but the men stopped her and took away her union responsibilities.

But Pregs was not to be stopped. She spent the next few years working to improve the conditions of South African women and encouraging women's organizations to unify as one group. She also accepted a job with the Women's National Coalition, where she could help to create a new constitution for South Africa—a formal, legal document that clearly describes the rights of all citizens and guarantees that all groups are represented. Imagine how important it would be for Pregs and the other feminists to have the rights of women included in a legal document. These rights included better paying jobs and a life free from gender-based violence. This section of the constitution was to be called the Women's Charter. During apartheid, such a constitution was not possible. But once the white Afrikaner government was ousted, a new constitution with a Women's Charter included came into law in November 1993.

A few months later, Pregs was elected as a Member of Parliament in the first post-apartheid government. The new president of the nation was Nelson Mandela, a human rights lawyer and freedom fighter who had spent 27 years in prison because of his anti-government activism during apartheid. It was a historic moment because Mandela became South Africa's first Black head of state. Naturally, Pregs was excited to participate in this new government where there could be real progress in solving the problems of women and people of color.

But there were still problems. For example, on her first day, one of the workers in Parliament tried to seat her in the section where the wives of the members sat. He didn't believe that a woman was actually a member of Parliament, although more than a quarter of the new MPs were women. Also, the Parliament building didn't have any bathrooms or other facilities that women could use. It was a "men only" building. In this new Parliament, thirty per cent of the members were women, which was one of the largest percentages of women in government in the world. But Pregs also understood that most of the women members of Parliament, like herself, were actually doing two full-time jobs: cooking, cleaning, and taking care of children at home, and being a government representative.

Until Nelson Mandela's new democratic government was elected, there had never been any money in the country's budget to help women. With her new power as a member of Parliament, Pregs began speaking with her colleagues who had worked for a long time to persuade them that the government needed to create a women's budget. It was a difficult job because many old-fashioned male members had never thought about the challenges of women with low incomes. Just as she had done many times, Pregs held meetings and persuaded members of Parliament that the budget was needed. The South African government used that budget to improve the situation for a while, but unfortunately, it was voted out after only four years.

Another issue that affected South Africans, especially people with low incomes and women, was the terrible illness of AIDS. AIDS, or acquired immunodeficiency syndrome, is caused by the human immunodeficiency virus (HIV), which was first diagnosed about forty years ago and spread throughout the world. In South Africa, many people were dying from the disease, particularly South Africans with low incomes, including many women. For about ten years, there was very limited access to medicine to treat AIDS-related conditions. During that time, in fact, more South Africans died of AIDS than from any other illness. So, when treatments were developed, Pregs fought to ensure that women and poorer communities could access medicines, not just the more privileged. She even was able to persuade wealthier countries to donate drug supplies. Incredibly, even though many South Africans were dying, racist members of Parliament and others were actually threatening Pregs in an effort to stop her advocacy. For example, one day a car was following hers at high speed, trying to cause an accident. Pregs had to call the police, who arrested the driver.

Pregs continued to work in the South African Parliament until 2002. In 2007, she wrote and published her life story, *Love and Courage: A Story of Insubordination*. Today, this woman with an independent spirit prefers to contribute in other ways. She has served on the South African Human Rights Commission, which investigates situations when people's rights have been violated and then brings them justice. Working as an independent writer and consultant has given her the freedom and opportunity to give her honest opinion about all of the issues that concern her. During the COVID-19 crisis, she constantly made recommendations to the government to protect all South Africans concerning vaccinations, masking, and paid sick days for those who became ill.

Pregs Govender remains a courageous "insubordinate" activist who has spent her life trying to improve the lives of women, those with low incomes, and all people of color.

LILY EBERT

USING SOCIAL MEDIA TO FIGHT ANTISEMITISM

Holocaust survivor Lily Ebert, who will soon celebrate her one-hundredth birthday, is an inspiring example of living history. For many years, she has been telling stories of her harrowing life as a concentration camp survivor and passing on survival lessons. Lily has recounted her stories of courage and resilience personally to three generations of her family. And because of all the new types of mass communication, these invaluable lessons have also been passed on to millions of others who may have never heard her story.

Lily Ebert grew up in a town called Bonyhád in southwest Hungary in the 1920s and 1930s. At that time, although Lily and her family faced discrimination for their Jewish faith and culture, Jewish people were an important community in the town and made up fourteen per cent of its population. With the strength of the Jewish community in Bonyhád, life was relatively happy and peaceful until war broke out throughout Europe. In 1939, Adolf Hitler and his Nazi army invaded and occupied Poland, acts that caused Britain and France to declare war on Germany and the Nazis. Hitler and his army continued to invade many other countries, eventually reaching Hungary in 1944. By this time, Lily was a teenager.

Hitler and the Nazis tortured, imprisoned, and killed millions of people, including Roma, gay men, and people with disabilities, but the group that they especially targeted was Jews. As they had done in every country they invaded and occupied, the Nazis in Hungary confiscated Jewish people's property and valuables and placed restrictions on their daily lives. Jews weren't allowed to leave their homes and were constantly being watched. They had to obey strict curfews that forbade them from going out after dark. Their cars and bicycles were taken by the Nazis, and they couldn't own radios so that war news was kept from them. Also, Jews were forced to identify themselves by wearing yellow stars that were sewn on their clothes, to be visible at all times. By physically marking them in this way, the Nazis wanted to make them feel like unwelcome outsiders to be avoided by all Christian Germans, including their neighbors and friends. The warning to all non-Jews was that kindness and support to Jews could result in punishment.

The occupiers enforced these restrictions and prohibitions, which rigidly controlled Jewish people's movements at all times. But Lily's mother was able to save an inexpensive gold pendant that she wanted to keep for her daughter by hiding it in her shoe.

Jewish people in Nazi-occupied countries were eventually ordered out of their hometowns, forced onto trains or buses, and deported to prisons called concentration camps. The Nazis sped up this process, imprisoning and murdering more and more people, as the war raged on. In July 1944, when she was twenty years old, Lily, her mother, brother, and three sisters were ordered to leave their town and were deported to one of these camps. Along with the other Jews in their town, they were transported in overcrowded train cars, which had previously been used to deliver cows. On these horrible journeys, the people had to stand for hours without any food, water, or washrooms, and often in terrible heat. Sometimes, older and sick people died on the trip. As the train approached the camp, Lily's mother told her to switch shoes with her. The precious pendant Lily's mother had saved was now hidden inside the heel of her daughter's shoe.

The train carrying the Jewish prisoners finally arrived in Auschwitz, Poland, which was the site of the most notorious death camp of the Holocaust. Lily was shocked to see that the prisoners were living in dehumanizing conditions. Many of them were so starved that they looked like skeletons and were dressed in torn, striped uniforms. Both men and women had shaved heads. As they were ordered off the train, they could see smoke coming from the chimneys and smell burning bodies. Lily then realized that Auschwitz was truly hell on earth. The Nazis had a specific selection process for the people they had newly imprisoned, so not all of the prisoners went immediately to their deaths. On arrival, they were ordered to climb out of the train and stand together with five people in a row. Then, the evil Dr. Josef Mengele, sarcastically nicknamed "The Angel of Auschwitz" because of his brutality, stood and pointed to prisoners, deciding which direction they needed to walk. But the Jewish people had no idea what would happen to them if they were told to go right or left.

Those who were sent to the left were told that they were going to shower together and then get new clothes. They were then ushered into huge shower rooms that held several hundred people at a time. Tragically, these "shower" rooms were actually gas chambers. Once the Jewish prisoners were packed into the chamber, the Nazis would release a pellet of Zyklon B gas into the room, killing everyone almost instantly. Their bodies were then burned in the crematorium near the gas chambers. Gas chambers and crematoriums were located in many death camps during the Holocaust and were the methods that the Nazis used to accomplish the genocide, or mass killing, of millions of people and to dispose of their bodies and any evidence of their crimes. That was the tragic fate of Lily's mother Bella and her two youngest sisters. Lily never saw them again. It was only after the end of the war that Lily found out that more than one hundred members of her extended family had been murdered in the same way.

Since they were at an age where they were able to do physical labor, Lily and her sisters Renee and Piri were sent to the right into the entrance of the camp. They and the other surviving prisoners had to endure endless humiliations. The Nazis were meticulous record keepers. When prisoners arrived, they were assigned numbers that were recorded in a book, along with their names, so the Nazis could keep track of the numbers of prisoners in the camps at any time. But if that weren't enough, the Nazi commanders of many camps tattooed the prisoners' numbers on the inside of their left arm. If Jews attempted to escape, they could easily be identified, captured, and brought back to the camps or shot. For survivors, these tattoos became lifelong reminders of what they had endured. So many years later, Lily willingly shows her tattoo to anyone who would somehow doubt the horror that she had experienced.

During this time, Lily's pendant became more precious to her than ever. When the shoes that her mother traded with her eventually wore out, she was afraid that it might slip out. So, each day she would put the pendant inside the tiny ration of bread given to her. That way she was able to keep the memento of her mother safe.

Lily and her sisters were imprisoned in Auschwitz for four months and then transferred to another camp, in Leipzig, Germany, where they were put to work making weapons for the Nazis. That factory was beside another infamous concentration camp called Buchenwald, so Lily and her sisters lived in constant fear of being killed.

In 1945, the Allied armies, including the United States, Great Britain, the Soviet Union, France, British commonwealth countries such as Canada, and other European countries, defeated the Nazis. One person's act of kindness during this time has remained a treasured memory for Lily. During the Liberation, she met a Jewish American soldier who wrote words of encouragement on a German banknote, some money that he gave her. The words of encouragement were, "A start to a new life. Good luck and happiness." The soldier didn't sign the note with his name, so Lily had no idea who he was and wouldn't find out his identity until many years later. But she wrote that after the horror of the concentration camps and the loss of her family, he was the first human being who was kind to them. To her, he was the first person who she believed actually wanted to help them.

Freed from the labor camp, the three sisters began a new life in Switzerland. Lily got married and had children. The whereabouts of one member of her family remained a mystery for several years. But in 1953, Lily was finally reunited with her brother Imre, who had been a prisoner in a Nazi labor camp. Because there were so many Nazi concentration and prison camps spread throughout Europe, it often took a long time to find any living family members and reunite with them. That experience was typical for many Holocaust survivors.

Lily, her husband, and her children immigrated to England in 1967. For many years, she focused her energy on raising her family, which now includes three generations: adult children, grandchildren, and great-grandchildren. However, Lily promised herself that if she survived the concentration camps, she would tell her story. Like all Holocaust survivors, she believes in the motto "never forget" and wants the world to understand and remember the horrible atrocities of that time. So, for many years, she has shared her memories with her large family, with countless school children, in the workplace, and with community groups.

Recently, Lily has found an important ally in one of her great-grandchildren, Dov Forman. When Dov was a little boy, Lily didn't tell him about many of her experiences of the Holocaust, thinking that he was just too young to understand. But one day, one of Dov's friends was visiting his house while his great-grandmother was there and happened to see the tattoo on her left forearm, which is a constant reminder that she is a survivor of Auschwitz. Dov's friend asked about it, and for the first time, Dov heard about her experiences in much greater detail. From then on, he has listened intently to her stories and is completely dedicated to bringing them to a much larger audience.

Like many teenagers, Dov uses social media, such as Twitter and TikTok. He had heard his great-grandmother's many survival stories and decided to document them. That mission became especially important when the COVID-19 pandemic restrictions and isolation prevented her from visiting him, and from sharing her memories in person with community and school groups, as she had been doing for many years. She was now over ninety-five years old, and Dov realized that it would be his family's responsibility to continue her legacy. The Holocaust ended over seventy-five years ago, and those survivors who are still living are in their nineties or older. Once they pass away, there won't be any living witnesses to this shameful time in human history. Dov decided it was time to use social media so that Lily could reach a much wider audience.

Remember the American soldier who gave Lily the German banknote with the message of hope written on it? Dov saw it in one of his great-grandmother's photo albums and asked her about it. When she told him the story, he decided to post it on his Twitter account. Over a million people saw and responded to it. A Twitter user who saw it then sent Dov a suggestion of the soldier's identity. It turned out that the man, Hyman Schulman, had died in 2013, but he wrote remembrances of his wartime experiences in many letters to his wife, which his family continues to hold on to all these years later. Dov located Schulman's family in New York and arranged for Lily to meet and talk with them on Zoom. For her, it was incredible to speak with people who had such a deep understanding of her experiences. The soldier whose kindness had a profound effect on her had passed away, but she feels a lasting connection with his family.

Since February 2021, Dov and Lily have posted more than 380 videos on TikTok where they currently have 1.7 million followers and over 25 million likes. In all of those videos, Lily is wearing the precious gold necklace and pendant her mother gave her. Recent events in the news have motivated Lily and Dov to believe that she must continue to tell her story. In the last several years, there has been an enormous surge in incidents of racial harassment, assault, and vandalism against many groups and in particular Jewish people. Any discrimination or harassment against Jewish people is called *antisemitism*. The Unite the Right rally in Charlottesville, Virginia, in 2017, which injured many and killed one young woman; the deadly shooting of synagogue worshippers in Pittsburgh, Pennsylvania, in 2018; and another shooting in 2019 were just a few incidents in which hateful groups and individuals targeted Jews. Schools have also reported increased incidents of hate against Jewish students. A film of the rally in Charlottesville shows marchers carrying lit torches and shouting the words "Jews will not replace us." According to worldwide statistics, antisemitic incidents and crimes have increased over sixty per cent in the last five years.

The people who commit these terrible crimes and participate in rallies are called neo-Nazis or white supremacists. They use racist slogans, symbols, vandalism, and violence to spread hatred. Their groups are very active on social media sites where they spread their messages to their followers and urge them to perform vile acts. Facebook and other social media are examples of platforms of free speech. Anyone writing in a newspaper, website, or magazine, or speaking online, on television, or on the radio basically has the right to say whatever they want, although in Canada it is illegal to promote hate in public speech. Even those telling lies and using hateful language can use social media because they are protected by law. There are even people using these platforms who are Holocaust deniers, claiming that the Holocaust never happened and that Lily and her fellow survivors are lying about their experiences.

People committed to social justice know that they must take advantage of modern technology to counteract and fight back against the growing racism and antisemitism in our society. With the help of her tech-savvy great-grandson, Lily uses TikTok to tell the truth about her experiences as a prisoner in a Nazi concentration camp. In hundreds of videos, Lily recounts the day-to-day life in those camps and her feelings about them. For example, she describes her arrival in Auschwitz and the feeling that she had "arrived in hell." In another video, she narrated how the prisoners were given so little food that they died of starvation. She describes the breakfast the Nazis gave prisoners in Auschwitz, which they called "coffee," but which was actually boiled black water made from shoelaces and belts that they had taken from dead prisoners. The video in which Lily simply lifts up her left forearm to show her tattoo from Auschwitz has had twenty-five million views. In it, she talks about her first few hours in Auschwitz, being separated from her mother and aunt who went to their deaths in the gas chambers, and then being permanently tattooed. At the end, she simply points to the tattoo and says, "My number is 10572. That is what I was."

World War II ended over seventy-seven years ago, and young people who hadn't previously known anything about the Holocaust have watched Lily's presentations and then sent in their own comments and videos. In them, they ask countless questions that show their eagerness to learn even more about her Holocaust experiences and what they can do about eliminating antisemitism and other forms of racism in the world.

Lily and Dov have also collaborated with various departments of the British government to develop programs on Holocaust education. She has spoken to the British Parliament about the need to build a national Holocaust memorial and learning center. They have appeared virtually on many television programs in the United Kingdom and all around the world, giving interviews to 180 news programs in thirty-five countries. For all of her work, Lily has been given many honors. Perhaps the most important one to her as a British citizen was in 2016 when she was awarded the British Empire Medal for her work in Holocaust education and awareness. Lily was also one of only seven British Holocaust survivors who was chosen to have her picture painted and hung in the portrait gallery at Buckingham Palace. At the dedication ceremony of the portraits, Lily spoke with Prince Charles (now King), who was then next in line for the throne, who told her that it was an honor to meet such an extraordinary woman. He also learned that Lily and Dov were writing Lily's autobiography, called *Lily's Promise: How I Survived Auschwitz and Found the Strength to Live*, which was published in September 2021. Prince Charles was so impressed that he offered to write the foreword for Lily's book, and he fulfilled that promise.

At nearly one hundred years old, Lily would be forgiven for wanting to rest and spend time with her family, but she has remained dedicated to telling the truth of what happened to her and the Jewish people during the Holocaust. Her countless videos, interviews, and book remind us that we must learn from this atrocity and do everything we can to stop even the smallest acts of harassment and discrimination whenever and wherever we find them. In this way, everything that she has said and done is an amazing legacy to us all.

MARY TWO-AXE EARLEY

SET MY SISTERS FREE

As we get older, we naturally become more curious about our identities. As we celebrate holidays and other special days with our families, we gain a deeper, more complex understanding of our family history, culture, traditions, and religion, and we tend to appreciate them much more. We experience and witness life cycle events such as births, maturation, marriages, and deaths of those we care deeply about. If we're fortunate, older family members become our mentors, guiding us to that deeper understanding. They also relate fascinating stories about our ancestors, which enrich our appreciation of our place in the world.

But sometimes we are at risk of losing key aspects of our identities because of circumstances beyond our control. In some countries in Africa, Asia, North America, and Europe, people from specific cultural groups have been stripped of their identities when the government in power discriminates against their customs, religion, skin color, or political beliefs. These governments may stop them from living where they choose, getting an education, practicing their religions, having good jobs, and exercising their right to vote. Women all over the world have been denied their human rights and identities because governments and cultures consider them less worthy than men. Canada is an example of a democratic country that claims that people from all backgrounds are free to be who they are and celebrate their cultures and identities. Yet being denied her true identity happened to Mary Two-Axe Earley, an Indigenous woman who fought the Canadian government to regain her legal status under the Indian Act.

Mary Two-Axe was born in 1911 on Kahnawà:ke Mohawk Territory, a Haudenosaunee reserve near Montreal, Quebec. As a child, she lived with both her grandmother and her mother, who was an Oneida teacher and a nurse, dedicated to taking care of sick people in her community. As the original peoples of this land, there are Indigenous Nations and communities in every part of the country. Some Indigenous people live in urban centers like Toronto, Vancouver, and Winnipeg, while others live in rural areas or on reserves. Reserves are sections of land that were selected by the Canadian government for First Nations to live on. Following the early stages of colonization and the establishment of the British Dominion of Canada in 1867, the government wanted to secure ownership of the land out of fear of American expansion into the country. This resulted in a series of treaty negotiations between First Nations and the government. Although some Nations received payment for their land, it was typically a very small amount, and overall, this process of land transfer could better be described as a land surrender. Some reserves were created when First Nations negotiated these treaties with the government, in an effort to secure land, health care, and education for their people. But, even if a First Nation did not sign a treaty, the government forced them onto a reserve anyway. This was especially the case in British Columbia, where First Nations did not negotiate with the government and very little land was officially surrendered. The government took their land and made the Nations live on reserves without their consent.

Reserves are often in remote locations, far from cities and major towns. And contrary to common belief, the reserves are not always located on a Nation's traditional land and may not even be within the boundaries of the original treaty. Reserves are governed by the Indian Act and are under the control of the federal Canadian government. Importantly, the Indian Act states that only registered status First Nations people can live on the reserves of their community.

Sadly, when Mary's mother was treating Spanish influenza patients in North Dakota, she caught the fever from a patient and died when Mary was just ten years old. Following this, Mary went to live with her grandparents on the reserve. When she was eighteen years old, unable to find a job and worried about her future, Mary left Canada to live in the United States. She settled in Brooklyn, one of the five boroughs that compose New York City, where she had the support of other Mohawk people that had arrived before her. There was already a history of ironwork in Manhattan and a small community of these families from Kahnawà:ke called "Little Caughnawaga" lived on State Street. In Brooklyn, she met and married an Irish American man named Edward Earley, and they had two children. He was an electrical engineer and they settled into a comfortable life in New York. But Mary still kept her connection with her roots by visiting her relatives in Kahnawà:ke every summer.

For many years, she lived happily with her family in the United States, never suspecting that marrying a white man had drastically changed her life.

But by marrying a non-status man, Mary lost her legal status as a First Nations person because of a Canadian law called the Indian Act. Originally passed in 1876, the Act defines who has legal status and who therefore has access to the rights and benefits that come with it, such as the right to reside and live with one's community on a reserve. The Act also stated that any First Nations woman with legal status who married a non-status man, whether First Nations or not, lost her legal status and rights as a First Nations person. This had terrible consequences for many and created a category of people called *non-status*. Those who were non-status First Nations people are sometimes treated as though they are "inauthentic" First Nations people. Mary and her children thus lost their right to live in Kahnawà:ke, to vote in council elections on the reserve, to use social programs, to own or inherit property on the reserve, and to be buried on reserve land when they died. The Indian Act was unfair because the same rules did not apply to status First Nations men. They could keep their status, regardless of whom they married. Of course, this is a clear example of gender discrimination because the law treated men and women unequally. With the passage of Bill C-31 in 1985, which was intended to eliminate gender-based discrimination in the Act, thousands of First Nations women could have their legal status recognized.

When she was first married, Mary only cared about living a happy life with her family. But about twenty years later, when she was middle-aged, she realized that the Indian Act was hurting the women close to her. A friend of hers died of a heart attack in Mary's arms. That woman was born and raised in Kahnawà:ke, the same reserve as Mary. Her home was taken away from her because she married a non-status man, and Mary was convinced that her friend's death was caused by the stress of the shock she experienced from losing her rights and her home. She sadly said, "A law can make your brother discriminate against you."

Mary was so angry that she began to speak out against this gender discrimination. In 1967, Mary and Cree activists Kathleen Steinhauer and Nellie

Carlson started an organization called Indian Rights for Indian Women. This was a time of increased activism in both women's rights and Indigenous rights, and many groups were fighting to make their voices heard and have their issues addressed by the government. Mary and her colleagues made a formal complaint to the Royal Commission on the Status of Women, a government group that examined issues faced by women and recommended to the government ways to improve the rights of all Canadian women. Many people on her reserve didn't want Mary to complain. Men objected because they didn't want women in their band to have the same rights as they did. At this time in Canada and many other countries, the power to make and change laws was in the hands of men only. They usually did not like any changes that women wanted to make to improve their own position because they believed that their power would be diminished and threatened if that happened. Many First Nations male leaders did not want Mary to succeed in changing the Indian Act for another reason. They did not want the Canadian state taking over their community any further than it had with the Indian Act of 1876, a foreign form of government that took away their traditional form of government, removing the power of women the first time.

At this time, very few women were Members of Parliament and they struggled to get the support of male Members of Parliament to pass laws that would improve the lives of women. Mary actually began to receive death threats from those who didn't want the status of women to improve. She fearlessly ignored these threats, which came in letters and phone calls, during the entire time that she was working to establish the rights of Indigenous women.

Mary was determined and led a group of thirty First Nations women to speak in front of the Royal Commission. Their stories of discrimination must have been convincing because the Commission recommended that the Indian Act be changed. They felt strongly that both men and women from the First Nations should have the same rights regarding marriage and owning property as other Canadians.

Two years later, Mary's husband died, and she decided to move back to her family home in Kahnawà:ke. She had inherited a house from her grandmother and wanted to live there permanently. But her community's male leaders didn't want her to return. The Indian Act, which stopped First Nations women from owning or inheriting property if they had married a non-status man, still hadn't been legally changed. But Mary found a way to get around the Act by transferring the ownership of the house to her adult daughter, who was married to a status Kanien'kehá:ka man from the reserve. Although she could then move back to her family home, Mary was angry that she couldn't actually own it and thought of herself as a "guest in her own house."

Mary became even more committed to finally getting the Indian Act changed. In 1974, she started the Quebec Native Women's Association. The following year was the United Nations International Year of the Woman. Mary and sixty other Mohawk women from Kahnawà:ke participated in the International Women's Year conference in Mexico City. While they were attending the conference, the band council, the group of men who ran her reserve's government, voted to evict Mary and the other Kanien'kehá:ka women who had lost their status from their homes.

Furious yet incredibly courageous, Mary grabbed the opportunity to make a speech to this international group detailing the discrimination against her and the other women who had lost their status. News media from all over the world reported her powerful speech. The band council of Kahnawà:ke were embarrassed by this negative publicity and so backed down from their decision.

After many years, Mary's hard work was finally rewarded. On June 28, 1985, the federal government passed Bill C-31. This Bill made changes to the Indian Act so that women who had married non-status men could now re-register for their legal status. The week after that, on July 5, 1985, Mary became the first First Nations woman to have her status returned to her in a special ceremony. At this ceremony, Mary said, "Now I'll have legal rights again.

After all these years, I'll be legally entitled to live on the reserve, to own property, die, and be buried with my own people."

Mary lived in her house in Kahnawà:ke for the rest of her life. She died on August 21, 1996, at the age of eighty-four, and was buried in the Catholic cemetery on the reserve. This was her personal wish and only possible because she had fought so hard to regain her status. Because of Mary's fight, six thousand First Nations women and forty-six thousand of their descendants were able to do the same. That is only one of Mary's gifts to Indigenous women in Canada.

In 2022, a Mohawk filmmaker named Courtney Montour, who was working for the National Film Board of Canada, decided to make a documentary about Mary and the other First Nations women's struggle to regain their Indian Status. Growing up in Kahnawà:ke, Courtney has known about Mary since childhood. Although Mary died when Courtney was a teenager, Courtney was eager to make the documentary to bring attention to a First Nation heroine who seems to have been largely ignored by Canadian history.

The documentary about Mary's right to regain her status is called *Mary Two-Axe Earley: I Am Indian Again*. The title refers to the words that she wrote in her own handwriting once Bill C-31 was passed, when she and other Indigenous women finally regained their full status. In the documentary, Courtney interviewed Mary's son, friends, neighbors, and especially her First Nations sisters who worked side by side with her in their fight for their rights.

During her long battle, Mary frequently appeared on television, and her speeches to the Royal Commission on the Status of Women, Parliament, and other key organizations were often in the news. Sadly, most of this important historical video has been lost or destroyed. But Mary had also expressed her personal feelings and impressions of the struggle on other audiotape interviews that were recorded in the kitchen of her home in Kahnawà:ke and have been carefully preserved by her family. No one had listened to the tapes for over thirty years.

In the film, Courtney, Mary's son, and sisters in the struggle are sitting at her kitchen table in Kahnawà:ke listening to thirty-year-old recordings of Mary describing her thoughts and feelings in great detail. The recordings also reveal previously unknown facts about the Canadian government's discrimination against Indigenous women. For example, the government was so determined that the Indigenous women give up their fight that the Ministry of Mines and Resources sent them a letter ordering them off their own land. The government's reason for the order was greed. Their actual goal was to seize more land, to dispossess more Indigenous people of their land to take for the Canadian state. Some reserves have valuable resources as well. The government is able to do this because all reserve land is considered Crown land, held for the "use and benefit of Indians."

Perhaps the most shocking part of the documentary is that it shows rare video of then-Prime Minister Pierre Elliott Trudeau responding to Mary and the other First Nations women after they had spoken about being denied their status. The elder Trudeau had the reputation of being a champion of the human rights of many oppressed people. He was present when the women were recounting their stories of discrimination. However, rather than enthusiastically supporting their cause, he was arrogant and dismissed their problems. He responded to their grievances with these puzzling words: "You're equal when you think you're equal. If you think you're unequal, the law won't change that much."

Mary cared deeply for all girls and women. Today, First Nations girls and women are encouraged to register their status so they can keep their rights.

Since Mary's fight, other Indigenous women have led the way to protest and try to improve the status of people who have low incomes, people experiencing homelessness, and the environment. Mary's legacy is that now Indigenous women, as well as other groups in Canadian society, feel that they have rights and power to improve their lives. She is an example of bravery, determination, and persistence. Her achievements need to be recognized and celebrated, not only by Indigenous women but also by women all over the world.

CHANGING OUR CONCEPTS OF BEAUTY

Every culture has its own ideals when it comes to standards and definitions of beauty. Hollywood and the entertainment industry in particular present very specific images of beauty. Usually, these women are young, tall, and slim, and have brown or blonde hair, blue eyes, and perfect, unblemished light skin. When we are young, we begin to form our own images of beauty based on the people that our friends, neighbors, and families consider perfect and beautiful. These ideal images affect what we eat, what we wear, whether we wear makeup, and what we do with our hair. But it can be difficult, and sometimes impossible, to live up to these ideals, and they can hurt people deeply. This is why many people have challenged such beauty ideals. The three women in this chapter, Fatima Lodhi, Olakemi Obi, and Ogo Maduewesi, confront these ideals of physical perfection and are doing everything in their power to change their countries' ideas about beauty.

FATIMA LODHI

BEING DARK IS DIVINE

In many countries, women with darker skin live different lives from their lighter-skinned sisters. They are not considered as beautiful by society at large. Being treated badly or discriminated against because of your darker skin color is called *colorism*. In societies in which colorism is common, people with lighter skin are seen as more attractive, intelligent, and desirable. On the other hand, people with darker skin are considered unattractive, dirty, lazy, evil, and unintelligent. These beliefs about skin color have existed in different ways and at different times across the globe, but they have almost always been used to justify the poor treatment and exploitation of a certain part of society. The European and American enslavement of African people is one of the most significant and large-scale examples of the use of colorism. To convince people that it is okay to exploit and harm certain people, those people have to be made into villains or into people who lack the intelligence to know that they're being treated badly. One of the easiest ways to do this has been to take physical differences and make them into signs of value or lack of value, of goodness or of evil. With colorism, skin color is the main "sign" of a person's value.

In South Asian countries such as India and Pakistan, colorism is evident in the entertainment that millions of people enjoy on a daily basis. Bollywood is a huge industry that produces movies, music, and videos with South Asian performers. These films are popular all over the world. Most Bollywood leading actors are lighter skinned, while the evil characters have darker skin. The male heroes even use words such as *gori* to refer to the lighter-skinned women they admire. This ideal of light skin has a big impact on the lives of women. For instance, in countries such as Sri Lanka, India, and Pakistan, the parents of young adult men and women often arrange their marriages and look for partners who have lighter complexions. Darker-skinned women are treated harshly. If a woman with darker skin wants to get married, her future husband's parents can demand that her family pay them a larger dowry, a wedding present of money, jewelry, furniture, or other valuable items. In these countries, stores actually sell creams and makeup that are supposed to lighten your complexion to make you "more beautiful." Companies that manufacture these products promise customers that using them will change their lives. However, medical studies have shown that these creams can actually cause skin cancer and damage to the kidneys and nervous system in addition to the damage done to a woman's view of herself.

Fatima Lodhi is a young woman from Pakistan who is determined to fight colorism. Fatima was born in 1989 in Karachi, Pakistan, and raised in Islamabad. She is the first Pakistani on record to take a stand against colorism. She prepared herself to tackle such an important subject by earning a university degree in international relations and completing special courses to qualify as a social worker. Since 2008, Fatima has been working to improve the rights of people with disabilities in Pakistan and has volunteered for different local and international groups. She has also raised her voice to help burn victims, people with HIV/AIDS, and women who have experienced violence in her country.

In 2013, Fatima started the Dark is Divine campaign and website because she wants society to re-examine and change its standards of beauty. As part of her anti-colorism advocacy work, she conducts awareness and training sessions to help people understand diversity, learn to accept themselves, and develop a positive self-image. Through her movement, she is making two important points: society's standards of beauty are not realistic, and being fair-skinned does not make a person better than anyone else.

Different incidents in Fatima's life pushed her to start her anti-colorism campaign. In school, fair-skinned students were always treating their darker-skinned classmates badly. This behavior was also obvious among the teachers. For example, girls with fair skin got higher marks and won prizes and awards more often than those with darker skin. Fatima also observed that girls with darker complexions were less social and didn't go to many parties and other hangouts with kids their own age. They avoided outings because they were afraid of being bullied. Fatima herself was called rude names because of her dark skin. The lighter-skinned girls told her that she needed a makeover to be more attractive. When they gave her that makeover, she felt terrible because she didn't look like herself. She also believes that the television and other media that advertise skin-lightening creams are poisoning people's minds.

When Fatima started Dark is Divine, many of her friends were opposed to it. They knew that colorism was a part of their society but didn't want to talk about it. Fatima believes that young people especially need to accept that it affects their lives. Accordingly, high school and university students have contacted her to do sessions on colorism. Both young women and young men with darker skin have also started sharing their stories of discrimination in person and on the Dark is Divine website as a way of regaining their self-confidence.

Fatima is being recognized for her crusade against colorism. For example, she was recently honored with a Women of Excellence and Young Woman Leadership award in Pakistan. She has been interviewed by British television and different magazines from the United Kingdom, the United States, and Asia. She was invited to moderate a panel discussion at the International Women Empowerment Conference organized by the United States Embassy. Also, Fatima made a special documentary on the dangers of skin bleaching, which is a process of lightening your complexion. The mission of Fatima's Dark is Divine campaign to have people with all skin colors be valued and accepted by others is still growing, and she is making an important contribution in spreading this message.

OLAKEMI OBI

LOVING YOUR BODY AND YOURSELF

Popular entertainment and advertising content constantly shows us images of the "perfect woman." Most fashion magazines are filled with these images of ideal women who earn a lot of money and are famous for their appearance. But these images are created to make us feel bad about ourselves so that we'll buy the products that they're advertising, in the hopes that they will make us more desirable.

British Nigerian model Olakemi Obi is working to change the image of successful models and is encouraging us not to compare ourselves to them. Olakemi is a plus-size model, which is a term used in fashion to describe those who wear clothes that fall within a limited range of sizes. When she was in university, it was hard for Olakemi to find clothes that she liked and that fit properly. It isn't always easy to find stylish plus-size clothing in stores and it is often more expensive than other women's clothing. So, Olakemi ended up wearing men's clothes that didn't fit her properly. It can be hard to feel confident about yourself when you have to wear ill-fitting clothes that you don't like. But she developed a more positive body image when she saw a plus-sized model named Toccara Jones who competed on the third season of *America's Next Top Model*. Friends and family always told Olakemi that she was beautiful and had a strong presence. Olakemi decided to enter a few modeling contests and gradually became well known as a plus-size model. She placed in the top five of a contest for plus-size women called Ms. Curvaceous UK and has also walked the runway in several fashion shows. Her most famous job has been her appearance in a fashion show for designer Calvin Klein.

Olakemi's mission is to encourage women who look like her to feel great about themselves. In her opinion, it's far more important to focus on individuality and not compare yourself to anyone else around you. She considers herself a body activist who actively fights discrimination against larger people and encourages everyone to love themselves. In particular, she uses social media to spread her message. Social media is flooded with posts on how to improve yourself through fashion tips and various kinds of makeovers. Famous entertainers, actors, and reality and television stars also frequently use social media to communicate images of body perfection, which almost always means thinness. And even when we do see plus-size models, they tend to be white women. So, as part of her efforts, Olakemi has created a media campaign called Plus is Diverse to demand more diversity in the plus-size ad industry. Through Plus is Diverse, Olakemi portrays body types of women like her, which are not often featured on social media, challenging previous ideas of perfection and reinforcing the importance of including women of all body types. Olakemi is encouraging larger models of color from different countries and cultures to get involved as well. At the same time, she wants all women to realize that they are beautiful. Her website Plus is Diverse features women from all over the world to emphasize her point.

At the same time, on her social media accounts, she shows her followers how eating and exercise are connected with self-love. When we eat things that we like and that fuel our bodies, we have the energy for fun activities like dancing and sports that get our bodies moving and help us to feel at home in ourselves.

Olakemi describes her philosophy of true beauty as body positivity or, as she says on her website, "being audacious enough to love yourself." Body positivity can mean different things, but to her it means that we must accept, celebrate, and include in our lives people from all cultures and who are all shapes and sizes. Anyone who believes in body positivity refuses to make fun or bully anyone who looks different from them. It also means that if you are a person who doesn't seem to fit society's traditional ideas of beauty, you can love yourself and reject any feelings of not being "good enough" because of your appearance.

Olakemi's life experience has led her to have important insights and to embrace who she is. She understands that almost all women face many of the same issues around social expectations about their appearance. When people point out or make negative comments about the way someone looks, we may start to believe that it's true and feel insecure in who we are. Learning to appreciate yourself is difficult. Remember that other people's negative comments are not facts. Olakemi's advice is not to use negative self-talk. Instead, recognize that it is our unique qualities that make us who we are. When we do this, it's harder to compare ourselves to others in negative ways. Olakemi admits that this has not been an easy journey for her, and so she advises women to follow her example by looking for supportive groups that set relatable standards of beauty. Surrounding yourself with positive people who represent different types of beauty is one of the best ways of building your own confidence, as well as that of others. And when we feel confident, we don't need to compare ourselves to others. To Olakemi, "comparison is the thief of joy." We should only compare ourselves to ourselves, with the purpose of becoming better people.

OGO MADUEWESI

BEAUTY IS MORE THAN SKIN DEEP

Have you ever woken up one morning and noticed some blemish or other mark on your face or body that you hadn't seen before? We can develop skin marks or rashes for many reasons: food or plant allergies, an insect bite, a bad reaction to a medication, or simply pimples or acne. When we have skin problems, we might visit a dermatologist who knows their causes and can prescribe medicine or other treatments to clear it up. Eventually, the skin problem may improve, and we might feel better about our skin. But sometimes it isn't as easy as that; some skin issues have unknown causes and are difficult to treat.

In February 2005, Ogo Maduewesi, an African woman from Eastern Nigeria, noticed a patch of pink skin on her lower lip. A month later, a lighter spot appeared on the right side of her face. She thought it must be some kind of allergy and threw away the skin creams that she was using. But that didn't seem to fix the issue, and she began to see more and bigger white patches on the right side of her face. Her friends, family, and even strangers started to notice and ask her about it. Ogo went to the hospital where a doctor diagnosed her with a fungal infection and gave her an ointment to make it go away. Instead of improving, the patches spread faster on her face and then to her neck and hand. All the white patches were on the right side of her body.

Ogo visited the Lagos University Teaching Hospital, located in the capital city of Nigeria, where a medical doctor finally diagnosed her with a condition called vitiligo. Vitiligo is a chronic skin disease, which means that it is a condition that a person will have for most of their life. But it isn't contagious. The white patches appear in different parts of the body because the disease destroys the cells that produce melanin, which is responsible for skin color. Ogo decided to go online and learn more about it. She discovered that famous people have had vitiligo. For example, pop star Michael Jackson was diagnosed with the condition. He was embarrassed about it, so instead of talking about it, he hid it by wearing a lot of makeup and even bleaching his skin much lighter than its original color. Unfortunately, doctors have not been able to find a cure for vitiligo.

According to the World Health Organization, which focuses on the causes and cures of serious diseases, about one per cent of people in the world have vitiligo. Ogo lives in Nigeria, but the disease doesn't affect one nationality or cultural group more than any other. She is aware that people stare at her and others who live with the condition. She has even faced people saying thoughtless things to her. For example, people have asked her, "Who are the wicked people who did this to you?" speculating about an acid attack or a curse. Once, when she was in public, someone came up and touched her face, and she had to yell at him to stop. The man told her to clean her dirty face and she ran away in tears. One of Ogo's ex-boyfriends also broke up with her because of her vitiligo. At one point, she became so depressed that she tried to kill herself.

After being diagnosed, Ogo went to a dermatologist who gave her an injection of a medicine that caused bad side effects, such as stiff joints. He also took pictures of her skin but didn't really pay attention to whether or not her condition improved. Because she was so frustrated with her treatment, Ogo has decided to go in a different direction. She now focuses on eating a natural diet that includes more fruits and vegetables, but no products made from milk. She also takes vitamin B12 and folic acid, which are supposed to improve a person's immune system and help protect against infection and disease. Her condition has not gotten worse.

Ogo took some time to come to terms with her condition. Her Christian faith has been helpful in that process. Her pastor, or church leader, advised her that she should not give others the power to make her lose sight of her goals. So, she made the conscious decision to become more confident in the way she presents herself to others. For example, she makes specific choices about the clothes she wears. Instead of fully covering up her skin, she wears fashion that she loves and is proud to be seen in, and she is photographed with her vitiligo in full view. She has stopped allowing other people's opinions to affect her self-image and the way she lives her life. When she first started talking about the condition, Ogo's own father didn't want her to talk about it and wouldn't speak to her for six months. But since realizing the importance of her message, he has become one of her strongest supporters.

Today, Ogo calls her vitiligo her "white tattoo." She feels that it's important for those who don't have the condition not to pity people with vitiligo but instead have empathy for them. This is why she started using her personal experience to help others with the condition.

In 2006, she began holding support group meetings in which people with vitiligo could tell their stories. As well as affecting their personal lives, people with vitiligo also face discrimination and harassment at work. Being able to tell their stories has given them the strength to deal with the misunderstanding and cruelty that they face. In 2009, the group took the important step of registering as the Vitiligo Support and Awareness Foundation or VITSAF. VITSAF is committed to supporting people who have vitiligo in Nigeria and other West African countries. The Nigerian government wouldn't recognize vitiligo as a disease until Ogo decided to send the government photos of herself and documents of all the research she had done. The government has since recognized the disease, and VITSAF went on to create programs to educate the public about vitiligo. This is important because many people have incorrect ideas about the condition, and these ideas play a role in the poor treatment often faced by people with vitiligo. Ogo and her organization have also held events to raise money for research and done awareness programs on the radio and social media. In 2012, VITSAF hosted the first African Vitiligo Conference, which featured experts from all over the world. Ogo herself hosts a fashion show once a year called VOGO, where the models are all people with vitiligo.

In 2014, VITSAF was successful in creating World Vitiligo Day on June 25, now an annual event. That day was chosen because it was when entertainer Michael Jackson, the most famous person with the condition, died. The event's first slogan was "No cure. Don't care. I am confident in the skin I'm in," which was designed to encourage people with vitiligo to be proud and confident. Since then, many have posted their pictures without makeup or other cover-ups on social media. In the same year, Ogo was given an Emerging Leader award by TechWomen, an American telecommunications organization.

Ogo continues to work tirelessly to help people with vitiligo. She has three important goals in building VITSAF. First, she wants to create more aware-ness and acceptance of the condition and to prevent other people from getting the wrong diagnosis as she did. Second, superstition is still a part of African culture and vitiligo and other skin conditions are sometimes considered pun-ishments for past sins. Ogo has made it her mission to inform and educate that it is strictly a medical condition and not a punishment. Third, she wants the health care system to take people with vitiligo more seriously and provide bet-ter treatment and more accurate information. For example, it's very important to tell people with the condition that they are much more likely than the aver-age person to get skin cancer if they spend time in the sun. She is encouraging companies to develop more products to help manage the condition alongside regular skin care. While we don't know whether a complete cure will ever be created, what is certain is that Ogo is using her well-earned self-confidence to educate and improve many people's lives.

CLARA HUGHES

RACING THROUGH LIFE'S CHALLENGES

When you think of an athlete who becomes an Olympic medalist, you probably imagine someone with a trained, disciplined body and fierce mental attitude. She always has clear goals and lives a healthy, balanced life, with a family who supports her every step of the way. But sometimes, great athletes come from challenging backgrounds and face enormous obstacles yet emerge from them stronger and better people. Overcoming their personal struggles makes them champions in many different ways.

Clara Hughes is an extraordinary Canadian athlete. She competed in six Olympics and won a total of six medals in two different sports: speed skating and cycling. In fact, she is the only Canadian athlete ever to win medals in both the Summer and the Winter Games. With her broad smile and outgoing personality, Clara seems like the perfect Olympic hero whose example every young person should follow. But nobody is that perfect.

Clara was born and raised in Winnipeg, Manitoba, in what seemed to be a typical family, which included her parents and an older sister, Dodie. But that family atmosphere was very troubled. Kenneth Hughes's home was a hard place to live in. He drank alcohol to deal with his anger and frustration and was a moody, inflexible man who tried to control his wife and daughters using many rigid rules. Clara and Dodie had to remain quiet most of the time, or their father would yell at them. He would also become angry with her mother whenever she did or said something that he didn't like. By the time Clara was nine years old, her parents were separated, and her father lived in his own apartment.

Clara's mother, Maureen Hughes, became a single parent who encouraged her daughters' creativity. She took them to art shows and introduced them to a variety of music. But no matter how hard she tried to influence them to have a healthy life, Clara had already embarked on a disturbing path. When she was eight years old, she would buy cigarettes, pretending that they were for her mother, using a letter she wrote and signed with her mother's forged signature. Then, she smoked the cigarettes herself. Because she saw her sister do it, Clara and a friend tried shoplifting from stores but kept getting caught. She switched to stealing money from her parents and grandmother. She also followed her older sister Dodie's example by starting to drink alcohol heavily at thirteen years old.

Even in her early teens, Clara was a strong, mature-looking girl who easily passed for eighteen. So, she bought fake identification from a boy at school and used it to buy alcohol. Clara started going to drinking parties with school friends, but then began skipping classes and hanging out with kids she met on the street. With them, she continued to party, drinking and smoking cigarettes and marijuana. The troubled teenager thought she was doing all of these things to have a good time and be like her older sister. But she was actually trying to escape a miserable home life and a poor self-image.

Although he was a negative influence in her life, Clara's father was also responsible for beginning her journey to becoming an elite athlete. When he was still living in the family home, Kenneth Hughes built a small ice rink in their backyard, which is where Clara first learned to skate. She was a natural athlete who won her first speed-skating competition in high school. In 1988, when she was fifteen years old, Clara was watching the Winter Olympics from Calgary and her attention was focused on Canadian speed-skating legend, Gaétan Boucher, competing in the last race of his career, the 1,500 meters. Boucher had already won multiple medals in three Olympic Games. Clara was mesmerized by Boucher's amazing athletic ability, determination, and joy as he raced one last time. He crossed the finish line in ninth place and so didn't win a medal. But what impressed Clara was Boucher's exhilaration in skating with all of his heart.

The next day, Clara told her mother that she wanted to skate in the Olympics. Maureen was so happy that her daughter had a positive goal that she enrolled her in a speed-skating club headed by Peter Williamson, an inspirational coach who had been a member of the same 1988 Winter Olympic team as Gaétan Boucher. The coach told Clara to cut down on her smoking and drinking, and to attend school regularly. For the first time, she earned As in her classes, and was surrounded by new friends, her speed-skating teammates, who were focused on setting and achieving goals. Training with them every day, Clara learned a new respect for herself and her abilities. Unfortunately, her coach accepted a new job in another city, leaving her feeling lost and unsure of her future.

Clara is such a naturally gifted athlete that she became a champion in another sport: cycling. She got her first two-wheel bike when she was six years old, never even needing training wheels. Once her speed-skating coach left, Clara accepted the challenge of becoming a champion cyclist. At eighteen, she was invited by a coach named Mirek Mazur to train with him. Clara had always loved speed and thought that as a speed skater, she could only be successful competing in short, fast races. But her new coach's methods helped her understand that she could also be a great endurance athlete. She started learning to pace herself to compete in long-distance indoor track races, outdoor road races, and team pursuits. Becoming so well-conditioned gave Clara great confidence and versatility, which ultimately allowed her to compete in six Olympic Games and many professional road races for almost twenty years.

When Clara was nineteen, Mirek Mazur moved to another province in Canada. He invited her to join him there and she agreed, believing that getting away from her family would be healthy for her. Also, Mirek was becoming an increasingly important influence in her life. She had faith that he was motivating her to be a successful athlete. They traveled to different places to train and compete in cycling races. It was the first time that she had earned a good living because cyclists who won or placed well in their races earned prize money. But working with Mirek also had its drawbacks. Very often, the training locations were small, isolated towns or villages, where young Clara felt lonely and depressed. Also, Mirek's methods were extremely strict, and she was forced to train long, hard days for eleven months a year, with no opportunity to relax. Elite athletes often become injured while training and competing, which they accept as part of their lives. But Mirek trained Clara so hard that she developed tendonitis and a painful hip injury that kept reoccurring throughout her long career.

Mirek also bullied Clara about her weight, telling her that she was too heavy to ever become a winner. He forced her to walk two hours every day before breakfast to decrease her appetite and burn extra calories. Because she was so afraid of gaining weight and disappointing her coach, Clara developed a serious eating disorder. She would binge on junk like cookies and ice cream instead of fueling her body with nutritious food. Then, feeling guilty, she often starved herself just before key races. Eating disorders are common among women in sports when they are expected to maintain a strict weight. Responsible coaches recognize this behavior and get athletes the help they need to recover. But Mirek only cared that the methods that Clara was using, as he percieved it, were helping her to win, and he ignored the damage she was doing to her body. Even though she was rapidly becoming a champion cyclist, Clara's feelings about herself as a person and an athlete were negative.

"Sadly, [cycling] made me feel like garbage even when I won. I was rotting from the inside," Clara wrote in her memoir, *Open Heart, Open Mind*.

Clara won many world and Olympic medals and a lot of prize money as a cyclist but often felt depressed after her races. The pattern of binging, starving, and self-sabotage repeated itself throughout her career. Whenever she won or medaled in races, Clara would stand on podiums smiling for photographers and fans. But in her heart, she never felt deserving of the medals and praise showered on her.

In addition to her own experiences, Clara witnessed other negative aspects of sports. When she was competing in races in Europe, many of her competitors were *doping*, using illegal drugs to make them stronger and faster. They could be taking pills, injecting substances through needles into their bodies, or even taking hormones or other substances to alter their blood chemistry. Of course, doping would give them an unfair advantage over other athletes. Dopers go to these extreme measures for obvious reasons. Being a professional cyclist is a full-time, stressful job, and winning athletes earn a lot of money. Although she sometimes struggled in training and competition, Clara never used drugs to improve her own chances of winning.

She also became very aware of other dangers of competition, especially in long-distance road races. Races throughout Europe are held on winding country roads and main city streets. Racers have to worry not only about crashing into their competitors but also about being hit by cars that constantly pass them at much higher speeds. Clara and her competitors were often injured but rarely allowed to stop racing long enough to heal. Clara felt trapped in a lifestyle she grew to hate but didn't have the strength to escape. Even though she rarely let anyone know how she felt, she struggled with many personal demons.

Despite her doubts, Clara was successful at the Olympics. She won her first cycling medal, a bronze for third place, at the 1996 Summer Olympics in Atlanta, Georgia. The event was a grueling 104-kilometer road race through the streets of the city. That medal was followed by another bronze in a much shorter race. Suddenly, at twenty-one years old, Clara became famous. But even being a double Olympic medal winner did not make her happy. To please her demanding coach, she starved herself before each race, sometimes eating only jellybeans and drinking water. After the Olympics, she returned to her destructive pattern of drinking, overeating, and taking recreational drugs. She became very depressed and didn't know what direction her life would take.

Fortunately, after those Olympics, two things happened that helped Clara cope better with the pressures of her stressful life and career. First, she met Peter Guzman, an intelligent, compassionate man, who she eventually married. While Clara was training and competing in both sports, she and Peter spent long periods of time apart, but their marriage is strong, and they are still together today. Peter and his family, so different from Clara's own, have made Clara feel loved and appreciated. His parents were loving people who themselves had a long marriage, and they brought this sense of stability to their extended family. Peter himself is fit and athletic. He spends a lot of time outdoors hiking, canoeing, and exploring many parts of Canada and the world. As Clara spent more time with Peter experiencing nature, she has learned a great love and respect for her surroundings. He has also given Clara the vital emotional support that she craved.

In part because of the positive influence of Peter and his family, Clara went looking for other methods to improve her mental health. For example, journal writing became beneficial in several ways. First, she used it to talk to herself, expressing any negative feelings that she couldn't share with anyone. In the beginning, Clara wrote about how she "despised" that she was abusing her body with her eating disorder. She expressed doubts about her talent and ability to win. She also wrote about her dislike of her cycling coach Mirek, who was becoming even tougher since she met her boyfriend, Peter. He hated and was probably jealous of Peter, telling Clara mean things, like that Peter looked like a "homeless guy." While writing down these feelings, Clara realized that her coach was at least partly responsible for her frequent bouts of depression, low self-esteem, and eating disorder. So, after the 1996 Olympics, Clara decided to leave him and worked to develop a more positive attitude toward competition, her life, and her mental health.

Clara gradually understood that she needed more support to heal her emotions and body. At a cycling training camp, she suddenly became very upset during a routine physical exam. She couldn't stop crying but wasn't able to tell the doctor the reason for her tears, only saying she didn't want to train anymore. She also continued to suffer from severe physical injuries. Clara decided that she would join her boyfriend Peter to rest in a remote town in California. This was the first of what would be several breaks that she took throughout her athletic career.

Clara decided it was critical to create a better balance between the high stress of competition and the life that most people have. She also began to view cycling in a healthier way. She and Peter took long, relaxing bike trips, exploring the countryside and appreciating nature. Cycling became a peaceful activity in which she could exercise her body healthfully and heal her spirit. Clara's tendonitis injury gradually healed, and she realized that there is a connection between physical and emotional health. She understood that when her mind was at peace, her body would heal faster. Taking breaks like these helped Clara regain her motivation to return to competition.

Clara returned to cycling with a new coach named Eric Van Den Eynde, who had a positive attitude toward training and competition. He admitted that her former coach Mirek had trained her to have tremendous endurance but had also worked her so hard that she burned out and didn't treat her respectfully. Van Den Eynde cared as much about her as a person as he did about her as a winning athlete and wanted her to be happy and healthy. Clara described training with Eric as a "gift." For the first time in her cycling career, she actually smiled during competitions.

As Clara was getting ready for the 2000 Summer Olympics in Sydney, Australia, a personal tragedy further changed her life and attitude toward racing. Like many cyclists who compete in long road races, Clara occasionally faced interference from traffic, crashed into other racers, and had even been hit by cars three times. However, in September 2000, a friend and former cycling teammate named Nicole Reinhart who was racing in Massachusetts was killed in an accident. Clara was in shock but decided to race in the Olympics in her friend's honor, wearing a black armband in Nicole's memory. She finished safely but without winning a medal. When she was asked about the race, Clara said, "I'm here to compete for Nicole. My victory was in not quitting. I'm proud of what I've done."

At the Sydney Olympics, Clara competed in another race where she finished in sixth place. Although she finished the games without a medal, Clara was not only happy with her performance, but also had a new confidence in her abilities and decided to return to speed skating. She felt that she had more to accomplish and was grateful to cycling for giving her more endurance and preparing her to be a better skater. There are significant differences between cycling and speed skating. For example, cyclists make a lot of money racing in professional races all over the world, but speed skaters are not paid to train and have to pay for the facilities and equipment necessary to their sport. Another difference is that speed skating is much harder technically.

For example, she needed to get her body used to the crouch, the bent over posture that speed skaters use when they race because it cuts back on wind resistance. Clara's training in the sport went very well, and she set her sights on making the Canadian speed-skating team for the 2002 Winter Olympics in Salt Lake City, Utah.

Clara qualified for that Olympics. Even though it was her third one, it was the first time that she was truly enjoying the experience. In her first race, the 3,000 meters, Clara finished ninth and was happy with her performance. Clara's new attitude was that she was just a beginner at speed skating again who was competing with experts, and that her finish in the 3,000 meters was an excellent preparation for her next, even longer race, the 5,000 meters. Clara won a bronze medal in the 5,000-meter race, and so became the first Canadian athlete to win medals in both the Winter and the Summer Olympics.

Clara's new attitude toward competition seemed to give her a sense of peace and accomplishment, but unfortunately that feeling didn't last. In the year before the 2006 Winter Olympics in Torino, Italy, she began to drink alcohol heavily, which would hurt her athletic performance. Leading up to the next Olympics, she also had fights with her coaches and her husband. Clara finally decided to see a psychologist who helps patients deal with their mental health issues. He guided her to understand that her self-destructive behavior was a pattern that would keep repeating unless she got professional help.

Watching other athletes use their fame to make positive changes for others motivated Clara. She first learned about an organization called Right to Play, founded by a Norwegian speed skater named Johann Koss, who won four Olympic gold medals. Right to Play delivers sports equipment to children in developing and war-torn countries. Then, she watched as an American speed skater named Joey Cheek won a race and donated all of his award money to that same organization. During the 2006 Olympics, Joey Cheek's generosity became famous. His original donation of $25,000 eventually grew to $500,000 because many other athletes followed his example, donating their own prize money.

From then on, she made it her mission to learn more about the organization, and Right to Play became a big part of Clara's life. Watching a TV documentary, she discovered that some Canadian athletes had already been involved for several years. The organization not only provides sports equipment to children in difficult circumstances but also gives them health care, nutritious food, and education. It encourages girls to participate in sports and teaches leadership skills to both boys and girls. Clara has traveled to countries like Ethiopia, Mali, Ghana, and Uganda to tell her story and encourage children to get involved in sports, set goals, and work to achieve them. She has also decided to be honest about her own mental health struggles. She visited young people closer to home in isolated Indigenous communities in Nunavut, a territory in northern Canada. Due to the ongoing effects of colonization, Indigenous communities are at higher risk for many of the same challenges that have troubled Clara's life: domestic abuse, addiction and mental health struggles, and poor self-image. Clara has continued to travel to many of these communities, spreading a message of hope to young people all over the world.

In 2006, Bell Canada, the country's leading telephone and telecommunications company, became one of Clara's sponsors, providing her with money to continue training and competing in both sports. In 2010, she was asked to be the first spokesperson on Bell Let's Talk Day. The campaign raises public awareness about mental health issues and encourages Canadians to speak honestly about their struggles. Bell Let's Talk raises money for mental health programs, care for people in need, research, and ways to teach employers how to help their employees when they have problems.

Since 2011, Bell has held the campaign at the end of January. Here is how it works. You can make a post on social media platforms such as Twitter, TikTok, and Facebook using #BellLetsTalk, sharing your own struggles or offering support or suggestions for others. Every time you send a message, Bell donates five cents to their mental health programs. Since 2011, 1.1 billion people from all over the world have participated in Bell Let's Talk. Every year, in the weeks before Bell Let's Talk Day, Clara goes online and on television and radio with public service announcements encouraging people to get involved. She also travels the country to promote the program and takes part in many outreach events to speak about mental health awareness.

Clara's effort to help people with mental health issues hasn't stopped there. In 2014, she embarked on Clara's Big Ride. For 110 days, she cycled over one thousand kilometers across Canada, visiting more than ninety-five communities and spreading her message of awareness and compassion for people with mental health issues. The ride began on March 11 and ended on July 1, Canada Day. Throughout her journey, Clara cycled through freezing cold and snowstorms, and she participated in 235 events in 105 communities. By the time she did Clara's Big Ride, Clara was not the young girl who had started competing in sports more than twenty years before but a woman in her forties.

A documentary movie about the ride aired on Canadian television, with an honest depiction of Clara's own physical and mental health struggles. At every stop on her ride, she shared her own background and listened to emotional stories from people of all ages who deal with depression, anxiety, and panic; domestic abuse; youth suicide; and drug and alcohol addiction. They also spoke about how doctors and other mental health professionals didn't take their illnesses seriously, telling them to just "get over" them. Through her work in Right to Play, Bell Let's Talk, and Clara's Big Ride, this extraordinary athlete has transformed herself into a humanitarian who is making a huge impact.

After her final Olympic Games in 2012, Clara retired from competitive sports. Clara is still very honest about dealing with her mental health struggles and the family history that contributed to them. Because she, her father, and her sister have all experienced addiction, Clara knows that she must always be carefully examining her own behavior. With support from professionals and her husband Peter, she focuses on leading a balanced, productive life. She still enjoys going on long cycling trips to appreciate the beauty of nature. After many years as a competitive athlete, Clara Hughes's famous smile no longer disguises her inner pain and conflicts, but truly reflects the happy, accomplished person that she has become.

ALICIA GARZA

USING POWER TO
CREATE POSITIVE CHANGE

Alicia Garza's mission is to help people and communities take the power they need to make positive change in their lives. In 2013, Alicia, along with fellow activists Patrisse Cullors and Opal Tometi, started the Black Lives Matter Global Network Foundation, a grassroots online platform that organizes Black Americans and their allies to protest police violence and racist discrimination against Black people. Alicia believes that the kind of people we are begins with the way our parents raise us, and her own life is an example of this. Her stepfather was a Jewish white man from a wealthy family in San Francisco,

California, and her mother was a Black woman who was raised by hardworking, middle-class people. Both parents experienced discrimination because of their religion and the fact that they were a racially mixed couple.

Alicia's mother was a strong, determined woman and an amazing role model. At age eighteen, she left home to live in New York City by herself. She worked as a secretary but eventually decided that she wanted a more adventurous life and joined the army at a time when there weren't many female soldiers. In fact, Alicia's mother was the only woman in an all-male department, and the other soldiers were always trying to bully and harass her. Every morning, as they were sitting around the kitchen table, Alicia's mother gave her daughter important advice about how to protect herself as a young Black girl. She made it clear that Alicia was as smart, free, and accomplished as anyone else, and she should never allow herself to be treated badly.

Alicia was a very intelligent child who taught herself to read at the age of three. One morning, she read her mother a job ad from a newspaper. Alicia's mother was astonished and decided that it was time to enroll her daughter in school, even though at that time children didn't start school until they were five years old. But when her mother took her to public school and Alicia demonstrated that she could read, the school administrators didn't believe her and thought that it was some kind of trick. To them, it wasn't possible that a three-year-old Black girl who had not been to school could read. Alicia's mother could see that her daughter was being judged unfairly because she was Black. She decided to take an extra, better paying but more dangerous job as a prison guard to pay for an expensive private school. It was important to her that her daughter got the best possible education.

When she was five years old, Alicia experienced a huge change in her life. Until that time, she, her mother, and her mom's twin brother, lived in a neighborhood of San Francisco with Black and Latino neighbors. But then, her mother and stepfather decided to move in together, first in an apartment and then a house in a neighborhood with mostly white neighbors. As a biracial child with a Black mother and white father and stepfather, Alicia felt awkward because she stood out from other kids at her school, who also came from much wealthier families. As one of only ten Black students in her whole school, she felt that her teachers and other adults treated and judged her differently than they did her white classmates. For example, one day Alicia's parents got a call from her school from an administrator who falsely accused her of smoking marijuana in the bathroom. Her parents believed her, but it was clear to Alicia and to them that she had been stereotyped because she was Black.

When Alicia was ten years old and being stereotyped in her personal life, she also understood that Black people as a group were victims of discrimination and police violence. In March 1991, a young Black man named Rodney King was pulled over by the police in Los Angeles. The police ordered him to get out of his car, and then four officers beat and kicked him more than fifty times. This violent incident was videotaped by a bystander and broadcast on television. Rodney King survived but was badly injured, and the four officers responsible were charged with the crime of assault. They were arrested and stood trial a year later, but the jury found them not guilty. Black and Latino people in Los Angeles rioted for six days after the verdict. The crowds were protesting the not-guilty verdict as well as rioting against the poor treatment of their community by the government. The government tended to ignore them except through policing. Sixty-three people were killed, and a lot of property belonging to small business owners was damaged or destroyed. Many television news programs began important discussions about the unequal treatment of Black and other racial groups by the police. This terrible incident made a strong impression on Alicia.

Like many preteens and teenagers, Alicia sometimes behaved inappropriately and upset her parents, especially her mother. But her mother chose an interesting approach. For example, when she found out that Alicia had started smoking cigarettes, she warned her not to smoke at school, but she was allowed to smoke at home where no one outside of her family could see her.

Even though Alicia's stepfather smoked marijuana, her mother asked her not to do that in front of other people. Once, Alicia shoplifted something from her neighborhood drugstore. Alicia's mother was angry and afraid that being labeled as a criminal would hurt her daughter's future. Her parents believed that the crime was so severe that Alicia was grounded for a whole year. During that time, she was ordered to come straight home from school every day and couldn't hang out with her friends.

While she might have "stuck out" at school as a child and teen, once she began studying at the University of California, Alicia's feelings about her place in the world changed. At university, she met other Black American women who had new and exciting ideas about race, gender, and sexuality, which influenced her a great deal. For one thing, Alicia came out as a lesbian to herself and the world. Alicia also understood that even though Black women come from varied economic and cultural backgrounds, they share experiences of racism and misogyny. She became excited, absorbing the fresh ideas of many Black American and lesbian writers, and those of her Black teachers.

At university, Alicia became committed to the advocacy and activism that would become her life's work. She volunteered at her university's health center, counseling lesbian, gay, bisexual, and transgender (LGBTQ+) people who were beginning to deal with their own sexuality and identity, just as she was. After graduation, she was accepted to a volunteer program called AmeriCorps, working with Black American teenagers in her hometown of San Francisco. She worked for a year in various roles at a health clinic, a violence prevention program, and a crisis hotline for people of color. During this time, Alicia made an important observation: All of the people she helped were Black, but most of the organizers and decision-makers of these programs were white. Often, she felt frustrated that, as a woman of color, she didn't have the power to make decisions and changes in programs that would help people like her. She wondered whether the white organizers could truly grasp the problems experienced by people of color.

Then, Alicia learned about SOUL (School of Unity and Liberation), a training program where she could develop the skills that would make her an effective community organizer. This program paired research with practical advocacy work. Two days a week, she would read about the social history and theory, and the other three days she would work at Just Cause Oakland, a grassroots organization in the Bay Area working-class community, and later at PUEBLO (People United for a Better Life in Oakland). She spent twelve to fourteen hours each day knocking on doors to meet people in the community, talk with them, and then invite them to organizing meetings where they would work together to make changes in their neighborhoods. She learned about their families, their goals, and their experiences. It was then that Alicia decided to devote herself to being a community organizer and advocate.

In 2005, she joined a small organization called POWER (People Organized to Win Employment Rights). She was assigned a community of families with low incomes in San Francisco where most of the residents lived in apartments. This area was being taken over by builders who wanted to tear down the affordable apartments and replace them with more expensive condos so they could make a big profit. This plan would force the residents to move from the only homes they could afford, causing some of them to experience homelessness. This area also had problems with water and air pollution, which are often caused by fast city development that focuses more on money than the well-being of its residents. Just as she had done as a student organizer, Alicia knocked on doors and sat at kitchen tables to talk with people, listening to their problems and persuading them to attend meetings where they could talk face to face with the builders who were threatening their community. Alicia and the other young organizers in POWER believed that this strategy would help the community to understand that they could persuade the developers to listen to them. Most important, encouraging people who would be hurt by this change to attend these meetings made them feel like they were a strong community working together and showed they had a voice.

Alicia also got involved in registering voters for an upcoming city election. When Black and other racialized people vote, the results represent the wishes of all citizens, which is one of the values of a democratic country. Sometimes, voters from Black, Latino, and other minority communities don't register because they don't speak English, are unsure of how to do it, or simply feel that their votes don't matter. But even more often, they are denied their right to vote by the government and elections organizers who intentionally give them incorrect information about election dates, make it difficult to register to vote, and put election polls in inaccessible places. This is why Alicia and the other organizers worked hard to register voters and to make citizens feel that they had the power to improve their lives.

Alicia also believes that it is essential to work with organizations that include people from different cultures: Black Americans, Latinos, new immigrants, Asian Americans, and white people. Working with these groups has helped her to recognize that she has also had stereotypes and prejudices about some of them, which required her to shift her thinking. One multiracial organization that she worked with for a long time is the National Domestic Workers Alliance, which organizes for better pay and conditions for cleaners, cooks, and other workers in hotels, sports arenas, and recreation centers, who are very often people of color. As she met with these diverse groups in community meetings, Alicia also heard them use insulting stereotypes about each other. Alicia's solution for community organizers was to get them to ask themselves and the people they're trying to help to explain why they have those negative images. When people are challenged to give reasons, they question their mistaken ideas and may change them. The result is that they develop a better understanding of one another. They gradually realize that their goals are similar and that they need to work together to be successful.

While Alicia's early work of speaking out and helping others could be described as advocacy, certain events pushed her toward activism and protests. On February 26, 2012, a seventeen-year-old Black American boy named

Trayvon Martin was shot and killed in Florida. His death was tragic. Trayvon was visiting his father when he went to a convenience store to get a snack for his older brother. When he left the store and was walking back to his father's home, Trayvon noticed a white man watching him. At the time, he was on his cellphone with a friend who told him to run back to the house. The man approached Trayvon, who asked why he was following him. After a short, angry exchange of words, the man shot and killed Trayvon.

The man who killed Trayvon was George Zimmerman, a Neighborhood Watch volunteer whose role was to patrol the area, keeping an eye out for concerning behavior and activities. Zimmerman was arrested and charged with second degree murder, which means that he killed someone without a prior plan to do so. In April 2013, he went on trial for killing Trayvon. Zimmerman's defense was that he thought that Trayvon, who was dressed in jeans and a black hoodie, looked like he was dangerous. From the way that he looked and spoke to him, Zimmerman claimed in court that Trayvon was a violent troublemaker. But Trayvon Martin wasn't carrying a gun or any other weapon when George Zimmerman killed him. Zimmerman, of course, was carrying a dangerous weapon. At the end of the trial, a jury acquitted Zimmerman, saying that he was not guilty of Trayvon's death. He was allowed to go free. That night, Alicia posted a "love letter to Black people" on Facebook criticizing the verdict and using the phrase "Black Lives Matter." Her friend, community organizer Patrisse Cullors, replied to the post with the hashtag.

The next day, Alicia discovered that her post had been read and liked by thousands of people. They could feel that something important was starting to build. Seemingly overnight, groups all over the United States were organizing protests about the verdict in major cities such as New York and Los Angeles. With activists Patrisse Cullors and Opal Tometi, Alicia created the Black Lives Matter Network to organize and guide protest. All three of them posted their own messages and began to do media interviews about this new movement and the issues it was highlighting.

To Alicia and the other Black Lives Matter (BLM) organizers, it felt like as more and more people learned about their movement, the momentum really began to build. Black Americans had long protested against the racist treatment of Black people by major institutions like the government, as well as by individuals. But for the first time in what seemed like a long time, the general public was not only interested in learning about the experiences of Black people but wanted to know what they could do to help end anti-Black racism. Soon, BLM quickly needed to respond to more violent attacks and injustices against Black people. A few months after George Zimmerman's acquittal, a young woman named Renisha McBride was in a car crash in the middle of the night. She knocked on the door of a white man's apartment asking for help and was shot dead by that man, Ted Wafer. Again, the man assumed that because Renisha was a Black person, she was automatically dangerous. However, unlike George Zimmerman, Ted Wafer was convicted and sentenced to almost twenty years in prison for his crime.

Shortly after, in August 2014 in Ferguson, Missouri, eighteen-year-old Michael Brown was shot and killed close to his mother's house by a police officer named Darren Wilson. Not only was he shot in the head four times, but his body was also cruelly left on the street for four hours before being removed by police. Once this terrible event was reported on the news, people from all over the United States came to Ferguson to protest police violence and anti-Black racism. The government sent reserve troops called the National Guard there to control them. They stood on the streets with guns and tanks, which were completely unnecessary against the protesters who weren't carrying any weapons. Nationally and internationally, millions of people watched this protest on television or online. Alicia came to Ferguson to see if she could help to keep the demonstration peaceful and organized. To her, it was clear that the government of Missouri wanted to stop people from protesting, although it is their right as citizens, specifically because they were Black and threatening the racist power structure. Alicia and the BLM organizers were very concerned that the tension between the police and protesters would become so bad that it would erupt into violence.

Alicia and the BLM staff organized a Freedom Ride to Ferguson to support the demonstrators who were already there and increase their numbers. They believed that if they could bring a lot of people to the protest, then their message about the injustice of violence against Black people would be even stronger. After speaking with community leaders in Ferguson, Alicia decided to create a campaign to speak to television, newspapers, and news websites to explain how people felt about Michael Brown's death. They also wanted local Black leaders to go on the Freedom Ride, and they communicated with leaders across the country to organize similar marches in several other locations. Alicia arranged the Ferguson Weekend of Resistance where different groups would have a chance to spread their messages of resistance to discrimination and violence against Black people. Alicia's goal was to encourage more people to join them. She did that by again knocking on doors, talking with people about their problems, and inviting them to attend activist meetings. The work that BLM did in Ferguson radically changed the protest because it brought together other marginalized groups to support the Black community, including LGBTQ+ and feminist activists. Alicia understood that for a movement to be successful, it needs to get the support of diverse groups of people who have had similar experiences and shared goals.

Since it was created in 2013, BLM has grown to include many groups to deal with challenging social issues. It has been very important to Alicia that the movement does not have one organizer or leader but many of them. This kind of decentralized leadership structure makes it possible for local leaders, who know their communities' specific concerns and needs, to make changes at a local level while still having the support of a national or an international network of activists. So, now one of Alicia's main responsibilities is to motivate new people to join the cause and to train them to become leaders. In recent years, she has been building a new project called the Black Futures Lab, which aims to help Black communities become more powerful forces in politics. Workers and volunteers of the Black Futures Lab interview people and collect information about challenges in their lives, such as obtaining health care, housing, and employment, or suffering police violence. Then, they take several positive steps to try to deal with these problems. For example, they bring aboard famous Black sports and entertainment celebrities and businesspeople to help train and mentor new Black leaders in business and politics. They also donate time and money to build Black-led organizations and support local candidates who are running for government office. To Alicia and the other members of BLM, getting more Black people involved in policymaking and elected to government is one of the best ways to get and keep power in the hands of Black communities.

Alicia's life continues to be productive and full of accomplishments. However, one event has changed her philosophy of life and the way she lives. Alicia's mother, whom she described as "her best friend," was diagnosed with terminal brain cancer. She only lived for seven weeks after her diagnosis, and during that time, Alicia canceled most of the activities of her busy life to spend time with her. During her last illness, Alicia's mother was well taken care of in a program called a hospice. Unlike hospitals, hospices don't have regular visiting hours, so patients' friends and family can stay with them twenty-four hours a day if they want. In the United States, people usually need to pay for expensive hospice care using their own money, or sometimes they may have health insurance to pay for it. However, Alicia realized that many Black Americans can't afford health insurance or that kind of care. So, because of this personal experience, Alicia is working with the Black community to get better health care. At the same time, she has also understood that she has to take care of herself. Activist work can be difficult and at times dangerous, and it can be disheartening to confront the trauma of anti-Black violence and discrimination on a daily basis. So, Alicia makes sure that she spends more time with her family and friends.

Alicia Garza is now a woman in the middle of her life who has already accomplished great things. She has been a leader in teaching and empowering Black people, women, other minorities, and those who are being discriminated against or feel they don't have any voice in society. All of her experiences have taught her that having power is critical to changing the way that people think about and treat others in society. To Alicia, having power means having a responsibility to improve the lives of others. She also cares deeply about justice and holding those who injure or kill innocent people accountable for their actions. Whatever she chooses to do next, we can be sure that Alicia Garza will remain a powerful force of social change.

ANNIE JIAGGE

CRUSADER FOR WOMEN'S RIGHTS

The modern-day Republic of Ghana has been ruled by multiple kingdoms and states over the centuries, including the Bono state, the Kingdom of Dagbon, and the Ashanti Empire. Starting in the fifteenth century, the region was colonized by different European countries until, finally, the British took control in the nineteenth century, calling the country the British Gold Coast. At this time, the mainly Black population was controlled by a government thousands of miles away in London, England. Life under the rule of a foreign colonizer was difficult for most people, but for women and girls it was especially difficult because the only future allowed to them was marriage and motherhood. As an agricultural country, both women and men toiled at the hard physical labor needed to run farms. Women also worked as craftspeople, making and selling weaving and pottery. As the colonial government began to build factories in the region, some people became quite wealthy from selling the goods that were produced by poorly paid women in these factories. The wealthy were then able to hire women to work for them as cooks and cleaners. In all of these situations, it was assumed that women did not have career goals of their own, but rather were always working only to sustain their families. This has been the case for most women and girls around the world, for centuries. Then, most girls didn't even go to school because the colonial government was interested in training only men for jobs that they needed to maintain colonial rule. Eventually, girls were allowed to go to separate girls' schools, but only to study "domestic" subjects like cooking, cleaning, and sewing, which would prepare them for lives as wives and mothers.

Annie Jiagge grew up during a time of major social change in Ghana. Girls and women still didn't have many opportunities, but Annie Ruth Baeta, born on October 7, 1918, in French Togoland, now Togo, was fortunate to belong to an educated, supportive family who encouraged her to achieve lofty goals. Her mother, Henrietta, a teacher, and her father, Robert, a minister, wanted her to have an English education so that she would be prepared for any career that she chose. She spent her childhood living with her maternal grandmother in the coastal town of Keta, in the British territory of Togoland. Annie's mother and grandmother were both strong-willed women who encouraged her to think for herself and stressed the importance of responsibility, perseverance, and determination.

In the early twentieth century, the most popular and respected job for an educated woman was to be a teacher. In 1933, Annie entered college and graduated four years later with a teacher's certificate. While she was still studying,

Annie and a group of her fellow students took a tour of the law courts, and she became interested in how the legal system worked. But, at that time, there were no law schools in the Gold Coast. Annie would have to wait.

For six years, Annie worked as a schoolteacher and then the headmistress, or principal, of a private girls' school. But in 1940, the buildings used for the girls' school were flooded and then completely washed away by the sea. The girls were moved to a nearby school for boys, but that building became overcrowded. The principal of the boys' school didn't like having the girls there and wanted them to leave. Annie also would have preferred to see her students in a new building but didn't have the money to build it. With real ingenuity and quick thinking, she approached a local church to raise money for a new girls' school. She suggested that the church choir become a drama group, which could rehearse and then perform a musical called *David the Shepherd Boy*. The production was so successful that they were invited to perform in major cities in Gold Coast and Togo and raised enough money to build a new girls' school in December 1945. Even as a young woman, Annie showed the leadership and persistence that would take her far.

After teaching for a few years, Annie became restless and decided that she needed more of a challenge. Unfortunately, her father had died, but she had strong support from her brother and mother. For example, her brother, Christian, helped her prepare an application to the London School of Economics, a difficult institution to enter. An incredibly ambitious student, Annie also enrolled to study law at Lincoln's Inn, part of the University of London. Annie's mother gave her some money for her studies and also helped her to get loans. Today, it is common for women to enroll in these demanding programs, and many law schools have equal numbers of men and women students. But when Annie began her studies, there were only three other women in her classes: two from Britain and one from India. Annie was the first woman from Ghana to become a law student.

She met with a great deal of resistance from her male classmates who weren't used to having women in their classes. They thought that her goal to practice law was unrealistic and that she would never graduate. To them, understanding and practicing the law was much too demanding for a woman. One arrogant, old-fashioned male law student offered to arrange for her to study to be a dress designer, believing that it was a more appropriate career for a woman. Annie told these bullies that she would return home to the Gold Coast if she failed her first exam. Of course, she passed that exam and all of the others, and they avoided her from then on. In 1949, Annie earned her bachelor's degree in political science and economics and the year after that, she became a barrister.

While she was working on both degrees, Annie volunteered in social work activities which she felt were in line with her Christian values. Being raised in a family that always supported her goals, Annie really wanted to pass on that motivation to other girls and young women. So, she decided to work in youth camps organized by the Young Women's Christian Association (YWCA), an organization that serves the needs of girls and women all over the world. In Canada, the United States, England, and other countries, YWCA provides educational programs for girls and women, and especially for those from underprivileged neighborhoods.

At YWCA facilities, young children and teenagers can play sports, get help with their schoolwork, find emotional support for personal problems, and even get job skills training. Another important goal of the YWCA is training future leaders. Young people learn discipline, develop new skills, and strengthen their characters through YWCA activities. While doing this volunteer work, Annie realized that many girls and women weren't as fortunate as she and faced obstacles to becoming successful adults. She believed strongly that there was a tremendous need to establish YWCAs in several cities in her home country. Even while she was still a student, Annie began amazing work with that organization, which she continued for the rest of her life.

In 1950, after earning her degrees, Annie returned home to the Gold Coast to work as a lawyer. At the same time, she led a campaign to establish a national YWCA in the Gold Coast and raised money to produce a documentary about the need to create a YWCA there. Because of her hard work and commitment in raising money for that documentary, Annie eventually became president of post-independence Ghana's YWCA for five years. In 1949, the movement toward ending British colonial rule had begun, culminating with independence in 1957 and the declaration of a republic in 1960 under the first president, Kwame Nkrumah.

In 1961, Annie headed another campaign to build a YWCA hostel for women in Accra, the capital city of Ghana. Annie had learned about a horrible incident that convinced her that there was a critical need for hostels. A young woman had arrived in Accra from the countryside for a job interview. After the interview, it was too late to return home and so she accepted an offer from a man she didn't know to stay at his home overnight. That man robbed and sexually assaulted the young woman. When she heard this story, Annie was so angry and felt that she needed to get the government's help to build safe, inexpensive accommodations for women visitors to the city. Many YWCAs in countries all over the world already had these hostels where women could stay overnight for a small fee, and she knew that the women in her country deserved the same consideration.

Annie went right to the top and spoke with Kwame Nkrumah. He promised that the government would contribute money to build a women's hostel. She also found financial support from private companies for the project. The YWCA women's hostel in Accra, Ghana, is still there today.

In January 1953, Annie Baeta married Fred Jiagge, and soon afterward, they had a child. The pressure of combining her career as a lawyer with the responsibilities of her home life was too much for her. In many countries, lawyers spend years working in the courts or do other kinds of legal work, and after gaining this experience, the government can appoint them as judges in different kinds of courts. In Ghana at the time, it was possible for lawyers to become judges very quickly as long as they had the right education. Annie applied and worked as a judge in four different levels of court, including the Court of Appeal, which gave her a wide variety of experience. She worked as a judge until 1983, when she retired at age sixty-five.

Even while she was a judge, Annie was focused on her great passion: improving the lives of women in Ghana and throughout the world. For example, she became a member of the Executive Committee of the World YWCA.

In 1966, Annie was appointed as Ghana's representative on the United Nations Commission on the Status of Women. She was able to speak about the gains made by Ghanaian women and to compare their situation with that of women all over the world. One issue that Annie realized was a problem for women worldwide was domestic violence. For example, she read a report of a man who killed his sister because she had an affair with someone who was not her husband. Her death was called an "honor killing," and Annie realized that in many countries throughout the world, men could injure and even kill women that they thought had brought shame to their families. The law in these countries never arrested or punished men for these crimes because they were deemed to be part of their "traditional" cultures, and therefore many powerful members of society approved of them. It was clear that women's lives were worth less than men's, and Annie was infuriated by the clear injustice in this particular case. The killer was never prosecuted.

As part of her work with the United Nations (UN), Annie then wrote the Introduction to the United Nations' Declaration on the Elimination of Discrimination Against Women. This report described the details of the kinds of discrimination experienced by women all over the world. The process of drafting an official UN document can take years and considerable patience. That document goes through many writing drafts and then it becomes a United Nations resolution, which is an official promise and commitment that all signing countries agree to. Finally, in 1979, the Declaration on the Elimination of

Discrimination Against Women was adopted and all member countries of the UN have been expected to follow its principles since that time. Annie's work on the Declaration has helped to improve the health, safety, and quality of life for millions of girls and women around the world. For this significant contribution, she was awarded Ghana's Grand Medal, the country's highest honor.

Annie continued her important work for women's rights both in Ghana and on the world stage, where she demonstrated great leadership in several capacities. For example, she served as the first chairperson of Ghana's National Council of Women and Development, which promotes women's interests and well-being. In 1975, she led Ghana's delegation to an International Women's Conference in Mexico. She was also a member of the United Nations Secretary-General's advisory group that planned the Fourth World Conference on Women in Beijing, China, in 1995.

One of the key areas of human rights that Annie was especially interested in was women's financial independence. Financial independence includes the ability to earn your own money and spend it in whatever way you choose. Women have always been responsible for having and raising children, taking care of their homes, and often doing additional outside jobs, such as domestic and factory work to earn extra money for their families. Sadly, in most countries, women are paid either nothing or very little for this constant physical labor. In these places, men are considered the heads of their families, and women are expected to hand over any money that they earn to their husbands, brothers, or whoever is considered the male head of the family. In many of these countries, the law doesn't even allow a woman to have a bank account or own her own property.

Of course, without their own money, women didn't have any power to pay for cars, homes, rent, or other key items, making it impossible to live independently from men. It is also harder to go on to higher education when you don't have any money to pay for it and must rely on someone else's permission. A woman without her own money couldn't start her own business. She would have to ask the male head of the family to either give or lend her that money, and that person could very easily refuse to give it to her. For women living in abusive marriages and who had no money, it would be impossible to leave, save herself and her children, and start a new life. Tragically, many women were and are trapped in these impossible circumstances, living difficult lives without having a chance to fulfill their dreams. Worse still, when women lack money of their own, they are forced to live according to the whims of men, who may treat them horribly.

With all of these concerns, in 1975, Annie organized Equality, Development, and Peace, a conference for Ghanaian women to share their views. At this conference, she learned that one of the major needs for women was to be able to get credit, meaning the ability to go to a bank and borrow money. This can help a woman to start a business, for example.

In Canada, the United States, and many other countries, women also didn't have financial independence or their own money until quite recently. Canadian women couldn't open a bank account without their husband's signature until 1964, for example. And it was only in 1974 that a woman in the United States could have an independent credit card in her own name. Before this, banks would refuse to lend women money to open their own businesses or for other purposes. Their excuse was that women had low-paying jobs or often didn't work outside their homes, which made it seem unlikely that they could repay the loans. So, a woman could only get credit cards and loans if the banks believed that her husband could repay them. Of course, women who weren't married didn't have that option. Canadian and American women's groups and other advocates put pressure on their governments and major banks to give women a chance for financial independence. Similarly, after Annie Jiagge heard Ghanaian women's stories about being unable to get loans, she pledged to donate seed money for the organization Women's World Banking and then followed through on her promise.

The group is based in New York City, but it has branches in more than fifty countries all over the world. Since it began, its goals have expanded to include helping women with their personal financial planning, setting up and operating their own businesses, and teaching them how to earn and take care of their own money. Annie served on the board of directors of the branch in Ghana, where other members of the board called her "a quiet heroine and a woman who understood the pain of women."

A devout Christian, during her lifetime Annie found time to become involved in other causes in keeping with her faith. She was the president of the World Council of Churches (WCC), which is a huge community of more than 350 churches and denominations in 110 countries. It represents more than five hundred million Christians. As the moderator of the WCC's anti-racism program for several years, Annie Jiagge fought apartheid in South Africa, which was the cruel system of discrimination against that country's Black people, and worked for the release of political prisoners, including Nelson Mandela, who went on to be South Africa's first Black president.

As her country's most prominent women's rights activist, she also participated in drafting Ghana's new constitution in 1991. In helping to write this document, she ensured that the rights of all women are clearly understood by all citizens and lawmakers, and that the law must be applied fairly to everyone.

Annie never really retired but in her later years loved gardening and raising chickens in her backyard. Although she passed away on June 12, 1996, Annie Jiagge's lifelong contribution to the safety, dignity, and human rights of the women of Ghana and disadvantaged people throughout the world is her enduring legacy. Other women in her country and throughout Africa have followed her lead and continue the struggle to ensure equal rights for all people. Certainly, her lifelong work and devotion to these important causes will never be forgotten.

ACKNOWLEDGMENTS

Thank you to the very tolerant and generous women of Second Story Press who always were encouraging and kind and never lost patience with my technological inadequacies, probably because they were used to my sister, who is also a bit dumb about such things. Erin Della Mattia is a terrific editor who made my work richer and better.

My gratitude too goes to my dear friends, especially Janet Jundler, Liza Tharrat, and Linda Wise who were always supportive and willing to hear me vent during the difficult time when I was trying to finish this book. My faraway cousins, Pnina Bat Zvi, Yehudi Lipman, and Bilha Asher never stopped cheering me on in their regular calls and emails. And thanks to the inspiring, world-changing women who are included here and to those many, many others who, too, deserve to be remembered.

ABOUT THE AUTHOR

Helen Wolfe's career spanned over forty years in publishing, social work, and education. Her extensive teaching experience was in special education, history, English, guidance, and English as a Second Language (ESL). For almost thirty years, her work focused on helping ESL adults to achieve their potential. Helen also authored over thirty teacher's guides to accompany books and a documentary for students of all levels and ages, with a particular focus on Holocaust literature and education. In 2011, Second Story Press published her first non-fiction chapter book for young readers, entitled *Terrific Women Teachers*. Her second, *Unstoppable: Women with Disabilities* (2021), profiles ten Canadian and international women with disabilities who have not only contributed to their respective countries, but changed society's perceptions of what a person with a disability can accomplish.